100 WALKS IN
Somerset and Avon

compiled by

GEOFFREY ALLEN

D1340649

The Crowood Press

First published in 1993 by
The Crowood Press Ltd
Ramsbury
Marlborough
Wiltshire SN8 2HR

British Library Cataloguing-in-Publication Data
A catalogue record for this book is
available from the British Library

All maps by Janet Powell

Cover picture by Maurice and Marion Teal

Typeset by Carreg Limited, Nailsea, Bristol

Printed in Great Britain by Redwood Press Ltd, Melksham, Wilts

CONTENTS

36. Compton Bishop 4m ($6^1/_2$km)
37. North Hill 4m ($6^1/_2$km)
38. Westhay Moor 4m ($6^1/_2$km)
39. Castle Neroche 4m ($6^1/_2$km)
40. Priddy Pools 4m ($6^1/_2$km)
41. Blaise Castle $4^1/_2$m (7km)
42. Dulverton $4^1/_2$m (7km)
43. Pinkworthy Pond 5m (8km)
44. Brunel's Bridge and Leigh Woods 5m (8km)
45. The River Exe 5m (8km)
46. Culbone 5m (8km)
47. Stratton-on-the-Fosse 5m (8km)
48. The Outskirts of Taunton 5m (8km)
49. Ashton Court 5m (8km)
50. West Bagborough and Will's Neck 5m (8km)
51. Northern Quantock 5m (8km)
52. Ash Priors 5m (8km)
53. Dundry Hill 5m (8km)
54. Badminton 5m (8km)
55. …and longer version 10m (16km)
56. Dunster 5m (8km)
57. Winsford Hill 5m (8km)
58. Castle Cary 5m (8km)
59. The Polden Hills 5m (8km)
60. The Doone Valley 5m (8km)
61. …and longer version 8m (13km)
62. Larkbarrow 5m (8km)
63. Goblin and Brockley Combes $5^1/_2$m (9km)
64. Lollover Hill $5^1/_2$m (9km)
65. Haddon Hill $5^1/_2$m (9km)
66. Cheddar Gorge $5^1/_2$m (9km)
67. Dunkery Beacon $5^1/_2$m (90km)
68. …and longer version 10m (16km)
69. Lype Hill $5^1/_2$m (9km)
70. Crowcombe and Will's Neck $5^1/_2$m (9km)
71. Horton Court 6m ($9^1/_2$km)
72. The Wellington Monument 6m ($9^1/_2$km)

Introduction

The Crowood Press are greatly indebted to our compiler who walked cheerfully all over the county researching the walks for this book. It must be borne in mind that while all the details of these walks (hedges, fences, stiles, and so on) were correct at the time of going to print, the countryside is constantly changing and we cannot be held responsible if details in the walk descriptions are found to be inaccurate. We would be grateful if walkers would let us know of any major alterations to the walks described so that we may incorporate any changes in future editions. Please write to THE 100 WALKS SERIES, The Crowood Press, Crowood Lane, Ramsbury, Marlborough, Wiltshire SN8 2HR. Walkers are strongly advised to take with them the relevant map for the area and Ordnance Survey maps are recommended for each walk. The walks are listed by length - from approximately 1 miles to 12 miles. No attempt has been made to estimate how long the walks will take as this can vary so greatly depending on the strength and fitness of the walkers and the time spent exploring the points of interest highlighted. Nearly all the walks are circular and offer a recommended place to seek refreshments.

We hope you enjoy exploring the counties of Somerset and Avon in the best possible way - on foot - and ask that you cherish its beautiful places by always remembering the country code:

Enjoy the country and respect its life and work
Guard against all risk of fire
Fasten all gates
Keep dogs under close control
Keep to public footpaths across all farmland
Use gates and stiles to cross field boundaries
Leave all livestock, machinery and crops alone
Take your litter home
Help to keep all water clean
Protect wildlife, plants and trees
Make no unnecessary noise

Good walking.

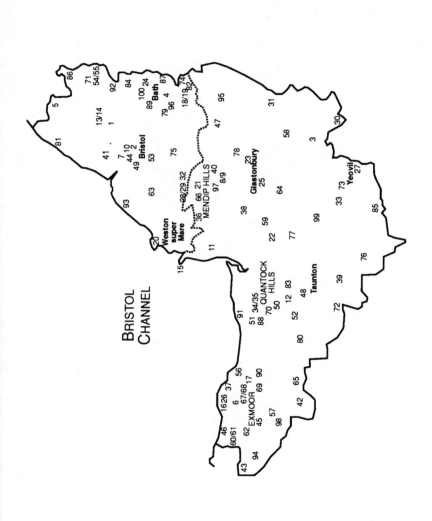

Walk 1   **THE RIVER FROME – ROUTE 1**   1m (1¹/₂km)
Maps: OS Sheets Landranger 172; Pathfinder ST 67/77.
A delightful riverside walk in an unlikely setting.
Start: At 638775, the Church of St John the Baptist in Frenchay.

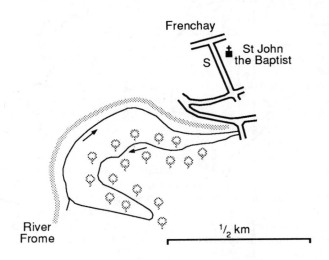

The Frome Valley is an extraordinary feature to be found so close to the centre of Bristol. The river flows into the Avon close to the City Centre but its final yards are underground and it is only fleetingly glimpsed as it emerges into the Floating Harbour through a portcullis below Neptune's Statue. Its line can still be seen hereabouts though – just look across the flower beds and wide pavements of The Centre. As an aside, the centre is not so called because it is the geographical centre of the City, but because it was the tramway centre, all city trams performing the loop around the flower beds, and passengers changing there for onward journeys. Later it performed the same function for buses and bus passengers, until it was realised that there was no reason why buses could not cross the city from end to end.

The Frome reappears – if you are walking up river – in Eastville Park and can be followed virtually continuously from there to Iron Acton, some 12 miles away. In the early stages the walking route is not always satisfactory, though in two specific areas it is excellent. One of these is described here: details of the other are given at the end of the route description.

For this walk make your way to the common beside the church by turning into Begbrook Park from Frenchay Park Road which runs from Eastville to the famous Frenchay Hospital.

From **St John the Baptist's Church** go south, passing the school. At the T-junction go right into Church Road, passing the White Lion Inn. At the next T-junction go left into Pearce's Hill, following it as it bears left. Now turn right into Frenchay Road, which bridges the River Frome. Go uphill, and look out for two paths to the right. One of these is the outward journey. The other the return. We take the second, which passes through woodland near old quarries. When a bridlepath is signed to the right, take it, following it through the woods. When the path emerges into a field follow the wood edge to a warning notice (riders beware of walkers!). Here follow the path down to an old bridge. Cross and bear right down into the Frome valley, forking right at one point to reach the river itself. You are now on the path back to the bridge. The river in this section is delightful. The lucky walker may see a kingfisher, as well as clumps of bamboo, and the remains of **Frenchay Mill**. When the road and bridge are regained, reverse the outward route back to the start.

The other excellent short walk along the Frome starts from the bridge at the bottom of Bream Hill (at 621765) where a footpath leads down to the river on the eastern side. From here a superb $1^1/_4$m (2km) walk – the distance is for the round trip, with return along the same path – reaches one of the river's weirs. This area of the valley is known as Snuff Mills.

POINTS OF INTEREST:

St John the Baptist Church – There are two churches close to the start. St John's, with a spire, is Church of England and dates from the mid-18th century. The church with the tower is Unitarian and is much older. The Frenchay area was a stronghold of the Quakers and other non-conformist groups for many years, and was, in the main, a temperance community. The White Lion is, therefore, quite a landmark.

French Mill – Despite its size the Frome was a real power house, running half-a-dozen mills and a foundry in the 18th century. The name Snuff Mills on the second short walk described above also dates from this era.

REFRESHMENTS:
The White Lion, Frenchay.

Walk 2   **BRISTOL – ROUTE 1**   1¹/₂m (2¹/₂km)

Maps: OS Sheets Landranger 172; Pathfinder ST 47/57.

A walk around the historical heart of the city.

Start: At Neptune's Statue, The Centre.

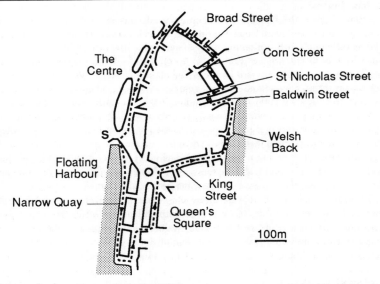

Facing **Neptune's Statue** go left, then right to take the cobbled walkway along the side of the **Floating Harbour**. This is Narrow Quay: follow it to the **Arnolfini Gallery** at its end. Go around the Gallery to reach Prince Street. Turn left, then cross over and take Royal Oak Avenue to reach **Queen Square**. Turn left along the Square's western edge, crossing the road at the end and continuing to **King Street**. Cross at the end to reach Welsh Back and another arm of the Floating Harbour.

    Turn left and walk to Baldwin Street. Go left, then cross at the crossing and go up steps to **St Nicholas Street**. Go right, then left into the covered market, going through it to **Corn Street**. Turn right, then left down Broad Street to reach **St John's Gate**. Go through, then left into Colston Avenue. Follow this through the City Centre, crossing Broad Quay to reach Neptune's Statue again.

POINTS OF INTEREST:

Neptune's Statue – The statue was cast in lead in 1723, and moved to its present position in 1949.

Floating Harbour – Prior to the building of the lock gates at the Cumberland Basin the Avon and Frome rivers – which meet close to the centre – were tidal in the docks area. The lock meant that the docks were permanently filled, a floating harbour.

Arnolfini Gallery – The Gallery occupies a tea warehouse built in 1830. The warehouse has been beautifully restored and now houses one of Britain's leading galleries for *avant garde* art, an arts bookshop and excellent café.

Queen Square – The Square was named for Queen Anne after she had visited the city in 1702. Prince Street is named for Prince George, her husband.

King Street – This is one of the city's most historic streets. Many of the houses date from the 17th century. Of these the Llandoger Trow – which now occupies 3 old houses of that vintage – is the most prestigous. The inn is named for the 'trows', old sailing barges that sailed to Bristol from the Wye port of Llandogo. The Theatre Royal in King Street dates from the mid-18th century.

St Nicholas Street – The church for which the street is named is now a brass rubbing centre. The covered market is also known as St Nicholas Market. Originally it was the city's fruit and vegetable market, but now offers a broader selection of wares.

Corn Street – The Nails, to the left from where our route reaches the street, are of bronze and were trading tables in the 17th century, the main goods traded being grain. Behind the Nails stands the Corn Exchange. It is believed that the expression 'cash on the nail' derives from trading on the bronze plinths.

St John's Gate – This is the last of Bristol's medieval gates, and dates from the 14th century. Elizabeth I is just one of the dignitaries who have passed through it. To the right, in Colston Avenue, after the Gate has been passed, is St John's Conduit which was one of Bristol's main water supplies in the 14th century.

REFRESHMENTS:
Numerous!

Walk 3   **SOUTH CADBURY** $1^1/_2$m ($2^1/_2$km)

Maps: OS Sheets Landranger 183; Pathfinder ST 62/72.

On the road to Camelot.

Start: At 632255, the church in South Cadbury.

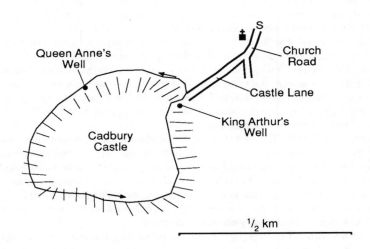

From the **church** walk southward down **Church Road** to a Y-junction. Go right, along Castle Lane, to reach a kissing gate at its end. Go through and turn right, taking a path around the lower slopes of **Cadbury Castle.** On the northern side the path passes close to **Queen Anne's Well**. On the far side from the gate climb up on to the ramparts and continue your circuit at a higher level. Descend to the kissing gate, passing **King Arthur's Well**. Now reverse the outward route back to the church.

POINTS OF INTEREST:

Church – The church is 13th century and is dedicated to St Thomas à Becket. The cult of St Thomas, the Archbishop of Canterbury who was murdered in his own cathedral in 1170, had reached its high point a century after his death, and many churches were dedicated to him.

Church Road – The striking building opposite the church is South Cadbury House, the former rectory, built, in local stone, in the 18th century.

Cadbury Castle – In 1514 Leland, the great Tudor traveller, came to Somerset and saw Cadbury Castle. He was impressed, describing it as "a very torre or hille wonderfully enstreightheid of nature". He was correct, though he might have added that the natural defences had been significantly enhanced by the work of men, the rounded hillock having had ramparts and ditches dug on its top and flanks so as to create a formidable castle. The original hillfort was Iron Age, and at its base was a prosperous town of wattle-and-daub houses roofed in thatch. After a fierce battle in 70AD the Romans took the hillfort and destroyed the town. The Romans built a temple, but the castle seems to have been of only minor importance. However, when the Romans left, and the British Celts regained control of their lands only to suffer a further invasion of Angles and Saxons, the hillfort became important again. The defences were strengthened, a timber wall was built on the top. But who lived there?

The hillfort was comprehensively excavated in the period 1966-70 by Prof Leslie Alcock who found evidence of a 5th century occupation by Celts who, at that time, were defending this area of Britain against the westward expansion of the Saxons. This is the time period to which King Arthur is usually ascribed and Prof Alcock has suggested that Cadbury Castle could be Camelot, Arthur's legendary castle. The idea was not new, even Leland had called the castle Camelot. The problem was, of course, that most people were looking for the romantic Camelot, the castle of the Knights of the Round Table whereas the real Arthur – if he existed at all – would have been a Dark Age war lord and as such would indeed have lived in a wooden palace in a hillfort. Is it therefore possible that the real Arthur rode out from Cadbury to defeat the Saxons at the battle of Mount Badon, halting their advance for many years until his own death as a result of treachery? Even the name Camelot could have a local origin – the stream that bends round the hill's northern end is called the Cam.

The castle is said to be haunted by Arthur, the King and a group of his men riding out along an old path towards Glastonbury on Christmas Eve. At the time of the full moon the group ride around the castle, then water their horses at Arthur's Well.
Queen Anne's Well – This fine old semi-circular stone well has fallen on hard times. It has a reputation for being a wishing well, and it is said that if lovers drop pins on to the water's surface and they float point to point their marriage will be long and happy.
King Arthur's Well – This brick lined circular well was probably the castle's main water supply. It is rumoured never to run dry.

REFRESHMENTS:
The Red Lion, South Cadbury.

Walk 4   BATH $1\frac{1}{2}$ m ($2\frac{1}{2}$km)

Maps: OS Sheets Landranger 172; Pathfinder ST 66/76.
A short walk in the heart of Bath.
Start: At Bath Abbey.

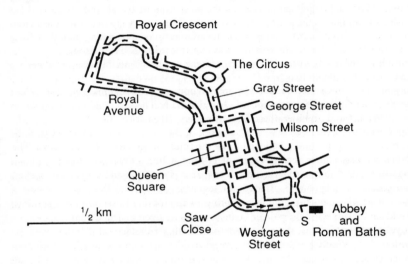

Walk along the northern side of **Bath Abbey**, then cross the road and turn left into High Street. Walk north to the first cross-roads. To the right from here is **Pulteney Bridge**, but you continue, taking the next left turn into New Bond Street. Follow this as it bears right (and becomes Milsom Street). Continue to a T-junction at the top of a slight incline. Turn left into George Street and at its end go right into **Gay Street**. Follow this to **The Circus**. Take the leftward exit from The Circus, Brock Street, and follow it to reach **Royal Crescent**, on the right.

Follow the crescent around to its far end then go left across the grass to reach Royal Avenue, turning left into Queens Parade and then right to reach Gay Street again. Follow the street past **Queen Square**, continuing in the same direction into Barton Street, then Saw Close. Now bear left into Westgate Street. Take the first turning right, then go first left to reach the **Roman Baths** and the Abbey.

POINTS OF INTEREST:

Bath Abbey – Offa founded an abbey at Bath in 760 and in it, or in a later building, King Edgar was crowned King of England in 973. Later there was a huge Norman abbey on the old site, the present abbey being built, in about 1500, on the space occupied by its nave. The design was revealed to Oliver King, Bishop of Bath and Wells, in a dream. In his dream King saw angels climbing ladders to heaven, and these ladders and angels are carved on the west front of the abbey. Inside is Beau Nash's memorial and the famous Birde Chantry. The chantry is a marvel of intricately carved stonework. So exquisite is it that the masons toiled over a long period, so long that Prior William Birde, for whom it was constructed, was bankrupted.

Pulteney Bridge – The bridge, which crosses the Avon, is beautiful, and one of Bath's most distinctive landmarks.

Gay Street – The Street was built by John Wood the Elder and his son, John Wood the Younger (!), leading architects of Georgian Bath. The son lived at No 41, while Josiah Wedgwood, founder of the famous pottery, lived at No 30.

The Circus – The Circus was also the work of the Woods, and took more than 20 years to build. It is widely believed to be the finest of the elder Woods' work. The Circus comprises three sections, each of 11 houses with a total of 648 Doric, Ionian and Corinthian columns in three tiers. The Circus is surmounted by a parapet with an acorn motif, as a tribute to Bladud, the legendary founder of Bath. Bladud, was a swine herd whose pigs found the hot springs while rooting for acorns. William Pitt, David Livingstone and the painter Gainsborough all lived in The Circus.

Royal Crescent – This, the most famous of Bath's architectural delights, was the work of John Wood the Younger. It comprises 30 houses complete with 114 Ionian columns and an unrivalled view. No 1 Royal Crescent is now a museum, the house having been restored to its 18th century condition.

Queen Square – The Square was the work of John Wood the Elder. Dr Oliver, discoverer of the Bath Oliver biscuit, lived at No 24. The plain obelisk in the centre of the Square's park was erected by Beau Nash in honour of Frederick, Prince of Wales.

Roman Baths – Not surprisingly the Romans utilised the hot spring, which delivers 250,000 gallons of water at a temperature of 120°F daily. The Romans built a superb Baths, complete with underfloor central heating and a sauna. The remains of these can still be seen.

REFRESHMENTS:

Numerous! Perhaps the best link with history is Sally Lunn's Tea Room in North Parade, on the southern side of the abbey.

Walk 5   **TORTWORTH LAKE** $1^1/_2$m ($2^1/_2$km)

Maps: OS Sheets Landranger 172; Pathfinder ST 69/72.

An easy walk – but only on Sundays!

Start: At 688923, on the Tortworth Estate.

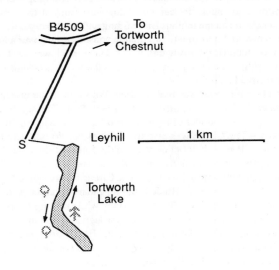

To reach the start of this entertaining little walk take Junction 14 off the M5 motorway, and then the B4509 road that heads uphill towards Charfield, Wickwar and Wotton-under-Edge. At the first sweeping left, uphill bend take the unsigned road to the right. Go through two gates, then past farm buildings on the right. Cars may be left near the wooden sheds at the end of the road.

The walk goes through the kissing gate by the sheds and follows a path through woodland to reach **Tortworth Lake** and its boathouse. Now follow the edge of the lake all the way round – the choice of direction is up to you. Reverse the start woodland section to arrive back at the start.

POINTS OF INTEREST:

Tortworth Lake – The lake is open for visitors on Sundays only: October to March 10 am – 4.30 pm and April to September 10 am – 7.30 pm. The lake backs on to Leyhill Open Prison, which is used to house short sentence prisoners and those nearing parole.

Tortworth Chestnut – The hamlet of Tortworth is reached by continuing along the road towards Charfield and turning off to the left. The church is soon reached, on the right-hand side. It is a quiet, pleasant building and next to it stands a quite remarkable tree. The Tortworth Chestnust is a massive spreading tree, nearly 60 feet around and thought to be about 1,000 years old.

REFRESHMENTS:

There are several pubs in the nearby villages of Charfield and Wickwar, but nothing in Tortworth.

Walk 6   **LUCCOMBE** $1\frac{1}{2}$m ($2\frac{1}{2}$km)

Maps: OS Sheets Landranger 181; Pathfinder SS 84/94.

A short walk around a beautiful village.

Start: At 911455, Luccombe Church.

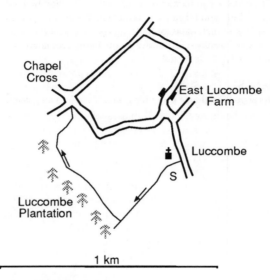

There is a car park on the village green.

From the church go out of the churchyard through the lych gate and turn right, passing several new houses and walking up Stoney Street. Just beyond Hill Gate Cottages there is a gate on the right. Go through on to a track signed for Chapel Steep. From this track Selworthy, a village which vies with Luccombe for the title of most beautiful Exmoor village, can be seen. Follow the track along the edge of Luccombe plantation, originally planted in the early 1920s as one of the first conifer groves of the newly formed Forest Commission.

    The track reaches a road close to the cross-roads at Chapel Cross. Walk to the cross-roads and take the road north-east for Allerford. This is Chisland Lane, and is followed to the next junction. Here turn right into Huish Ball Steep. Follow the lane past East Luccombe Farm to reach a T-junction. Turn left, and soon bear right on

18

lanes that return to **Luccombe** soon reaching the Green, from where it is a short step back to the church.

POINTS OF INTEREST:

Luccombe – The village was a Domesday manor, and has been a prosperous little spot for centuries, the local area being very fertile. During the Civil War the vicar, Henry Byam, was an ardent Royalist and tried to stir the villagers, who were Royalist sympathisers, into activity against the Parliamentarian troops who were garrisoned in Luccombe. Presumably he was successful, as the Parliamentarian commander decided to have him and his family arrested. The Byams escaped arrest and fled north to the coast. There the vicar said a fond farewell to his wife and daughter who boarded a ship to cross the Bristol Channel to Wales. Sadly the ship sank and both were drowned. Byam and his sons joined the Royalist army. The vicar served with distinction, eventually helping the future Charles II to escape to Jersey. At the restoration Byam returned to Luccombe, but in recognition of his services to the Crown he was made Canon of Exeter. As a memorial to his wife and daughter's death on the way to Wales he was also made Prebendary of Wales.

Luccombe church, dedicated to St Mary the Virgin, is in part 13th century, but has superb 15th century roofs. It has a memorial to Henry Byam, and a fine early 17th century brass of William Harrison. Church View, a cottage across from the church is dated 1680 and was the sole survivor of a row of thatched cottages that burned down about 100 years ago. In The Square the village Post Office is a superb building, and is complete with a Victorian post box. The name Ketner is a remnant of the time Robert Ketner, a shoemaker, lived here, about 100 years ago.

REFRESHMENTS:

There are none on the route. The closest are the seasonal tea shops in Horner and Selworthy. There are also inns and cafés in Porlock, and an inn in Wootton Courtenay.

Walk 7 **OLD AND NEW CLIFTON** $1\frac{1}{2}$m ($2\frac{1}{2}$km)
Maps: OS Sheets Landranger 172; Pathfinder ST 47/57.
A fine walk through the old town of Clifton.
Start: At the Clifton end of Brunel's Suspension Bridge.

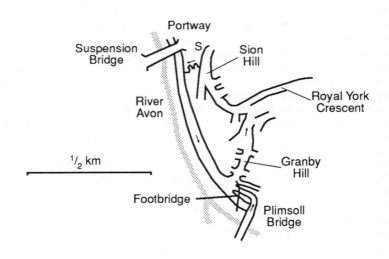

From the Bridge (*see* Note to Walk 44), go left towards the Avon Gorge Hotel. Before reaching it, however, go right down the zig-zag path, a wall-enclosed stepped path that leads steeply down to the Portway, the main A4 road which runs under the bridge. The path was constructed in 1829 to help Clifton residents and visitors reach the **Hotwells** by the river below. Those early users did not have to contend with today's traffic, so be very careful when you emerge – especially if you have children with you. Go left along the Portway to reach the **Rocks Railway** and **The Collonade**.

Beyond The Collonade steps lead to St Vincent's Parade. Take the Parade, looking across to the bust of **Samuel Plimsoll**. At the end of the Parade is Granby Hill. From it take the footbridge over the main road, to reach the lock in the Cumberland Basin. A better view of the area can be offered by following the main road and climbing the spiral stairway to the new **Plimsoll Bridge**. Ahead now is the Cumberland Basin, while back the way you have come is **Windsor Terrace**.

Return to Granby Hill and follow it past Cornwallis Crescent (to the right) to reach York Garden and **Royal York Crescent**. Now bear left past the Prince's Buildings into Sion Hill. Walk past the Avon Gorge Hotel and the top of the zig-zag path to reach **Clifton** and the start of the walk.

POINTS OF INTEREST:

Hotwells – The thermal spa of the Hotwells was opened in the late 18th century when spa towns were the vogue. Water from the hot spring flowed out at about 60 gallons/minute at a temperature of 76°F, and made this area of the Avon riverbed fashionable for a few years. River widening destroyed the first spa building, and by the early 19th century Hotwells had gone into decline.

Rocks Railway – The railway, whose bricked up portico is passed on the walk, was built in 1893 to link the tramway beside the river with Clifton. The ascending car was pulled up the steep rock by the descending one which had been filled with water. At the bottom the water was released into the river. There is talk of the railway being renovated.

The Collonade – This was the second spa building and dates from 1786.

Samuel Plimsoll – Plimsoll was born in Bristol in 1824 and is renowned for the invention of the line on ships which now bears his name. The line stopped the overloading of ships, and was responsible for a sharp increase in life-expectancy of merchant seamen.

Plimsoll Bridge – The bridge that bears Plimsoll's name was built in 1965 to allow continuous traffic flow when ships were passing between Bristol Harbour and the Cumberland Basin.

Windsor Terrace – William Watts, a local plumber living in the 18th century is credited with having invented the technique of dropping molten lead from a great height into water in order to form spherical lead shot. With the fortune he made Watts decided to build a wonderful Terrace in Clifton. Sadly the buttressing of the Terrace bankrupted him, though the resulting work, finished on a less grand scale, is still impressive.

Royal York Terrace – This wonderfully elegant crescent is claimed to be the longest in Europe.

Clifton – The old village derives its name from *clif tun*, the village on the cliff, a very apt description.

REFRESHMENTS:

There are numerous possibilities in Clifton village.

Walks 8 & 9   **EBBOR GORGE AND WOOKEY HOLE**   2m (3km)
or 5m (8km)
Maps: OS Sheets Landranger 182; Pathfinder ST 44/54.
Breathtaking scenery and historical interest.
Start: At 520485, a car park on the Wookey to Priddy road.

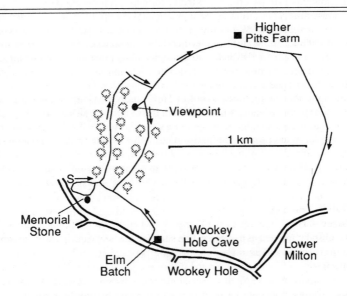

To find the start take the Wookey Hole road from Wells. Go past the caves – with
their ample car park to the left – continuing for about 800 yards. At a junction, go
right on the Priddy road which goes steeply uphill to reach the car park, on the right.

Go over the stile out of the car park, and down the stepped path, following red
waymarkers. Ignore a turn to the right, signed for the car park, but note it – both the
shorter and longer routes return along it. At the next path junction go left into **Ebbor
Gorge**, following the path to the top of the Gorge. There, at another path junction, go
right, still following the distinctive waymarkers. At the next path junction the route
reaches the signed West Mendip Way (*see* Note to Walk 66). The shorter route goes
right here, the longer one going left.

Turning right, the walker soon reaches a short, well-trodden, detour to the right which visits a superb viewpoint. Return to the main path and continue downhill – the path is steep, but occasionally stepped. At the bottom of the stepped section the West Mendip Way continues along the path, but our route goes sharply back right towards the Gorge and the car park. Walk back to the junction with the outward route and turn left. Turn left again at the path signed for the car park – as noted on the outward journey. Follow this path past the **Memorial Stone** to reach the car park.

The longer route goes left at the path junction. Walk uphill, then along the ridge wall, heading for the huge TV transmitter on Pen Hill. Cross several fields, passing south of Higher Pitts Farm, to reach a waymarked gate into a large field. Go half-right across the field to reach another gate. Go through and follow the path down through woodland. Exit from the wood and cross fields to reach the road through the hamlet of Lower Milton. Turn right and follow the road to a T-junction. Go right and follow the road, going right once more, to the **Wookey Hole** complex. Go past the extrance to the cave (to the right) and the car park (to the left) to reach Elm Batch (to the right), the last house in the village. Go through the gate – signposted for Priddy – beyond and follow the left-hand path up the field and through a wooded valley. You are now on the West Mendip Way. Follow it into the Ebbor Gorge Nature Reserve to reach the point where the shorter route leaves the Way, at an obvious Y-junction of paths close to a waymarker post. Fork left and follow the shorter route back to the start.

POINTS OF INTEREST:

Ebbor Gorge – The 100 acres of the Gorge is owned by the National Trust and is both beautiful and important as a conservation site. The limestone cliffs are an important area for flowers, birds and animals.

Memorial Stone – The stone records the gift of the Gorge to the National Trust by Mrs Olive Hodgkinson in 1967. It is occasionally called the Churchill Memorial as Mrs Hodgkinson gave the site to the nation after seeing the orderly crowds of folk queuing to see Sir Winston Churchill as he lay in state after his death in 1965.

Wookey Hole – Perhaps the most famous show caves in Britain. The Hole is famous for its 'Witch', a stalagmite boss that resembles an old woman's profile, for its remarkable collection of prehistoric animals and for its underground pools. Cave divers have explored these for many hundreds of yards. Also within the Wookey complex are a hand-made paper mill, Madame Tussaud's store room with heads, arms and bodies of the famous, and a collection of fairground items.

REFRESHMENTS:

The Wookey complex has all the refreshment possibilities anyone could require! There is also a fine picnic site at the start point car park.

Walk 10 **BRISTOL – ROUTE 2** 2m (3 km)
Maps: OS Sheets Landranger 172; Pathfinder ST 47/57.
A second walk around the historic heart of the city.
Start: At Neptune's Statue, The Centre.

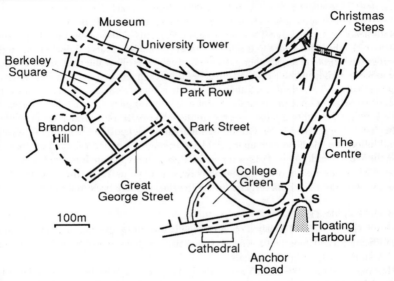

Facing Neptune's Statue (*see* Note to Walk 2), turn right to reach Anchor Road. To the left here is the Watershed, a complex of cafés and shops housed in Victorian dock buildings. Cross Anchor Road – look right! – and bear left to cross it again – look left! – to reach College Green. Walk past the **Swallow Royal Hotel** and continue to reach **Bristol Cathedral**.

Cross the road and walk around the crescent frontage of the **Council House** to reach Park Street. Go left and walk up the Street to reach **Great George Street**, to the left. Go up the street to reach, to the right, an entrance to **Brandon Hill**. The Hill is crossed by a complex of paths. Choose convenient ones to reach the unmistakable high spot of **Cabot Tower**. From the Tower head away from the entrance you used to reach the Hill, and turn right at the first path junction. Follow this path down, crossing to a wider path to reach a doorway in a wall. Beyond is Berkeley Square. Go down to the Square proper, turning left, then right to go around its southern and western edges. Cross the main road ahead – formed by the junction of Queen's Road, Park Street, Park Row and Triangle Street – by using the sets of pedestrian crossings. On the far side turn right passing the old University Refectory, built in the style of the Doge's Palace in Venice, the Museum and **University Tower**.

Cross Park Row at the pedestrian crossing near the Tower and continue along its southern side. Pass the entrance to the NCP car park and cross the top of Lodge Street and Lower Park Road. Continue to reach the top of a flight of steps to the right. Go down these to reach Colston Street. Cross, and go right, then quickly left to reach **Christmas Steps**. Descend these to reach Lewin's Mead. Turn right into the City Centre and cross this to regain Neptune's Statue.

POINTS OF INTEREST:

Swallow Royal Hotel – Once this was just the Royal Hotel. When the old building had become dilapidated it was recovered by demolishing all but the fine facade and rebuilding it. The facade itself has been repaired and cleaned.

Bristol Cathedral – The first Cathedral building here was begun in the mid-12th century, though the site is an ancient one, with Christian associations going back to the 7th century. But though the Cathedral is Norman in origin, building work continued until the 19th century.

Council House – The council offices, built in the form of one of the great crescents of Clifton and Bath, was opened by Queen Elizabeth II in 1956.

Great George Street – This fine street is set off by the Neo-Classical St George's Chapel, now deconsecrated and used as a concert hall.

Brandon Hill – Bristol is very proud of its green spaces, and the walker will meet many city dwellers taking the air and admiring the view from the Hill. Interestingly, city folk still have the right to dry clothes and beat carpets on the Hill.

Cabot Tower – The Tower was erected in 1897, the 400th anniversary of John Cabot's voyage from Bristol to Newfoundland. From it there is a superb view of the city, and of the SS Great Britain, built in the city in 1843, but now one of its most recent landmarks.

University Tower – The city's most distinctive landmark – after Brunel's bridge – was built in 1925 and is 215 feet (65metres) tall.

Christmas Steps – The steps were built in 1669 to save further injuries on the steep path down to what was then the river bank. They are still lit by gas lamps.

REFRESHMENTS:
Numerous!

Walk 11   **BRENT KNOLL**   2m (3km)

Maps: OS Sheets Landranger 182; Pathfinder ST 25/35.
A quick trip up a distinctive landmark.
Start: At 343519, St Mary's Church, East Brent.

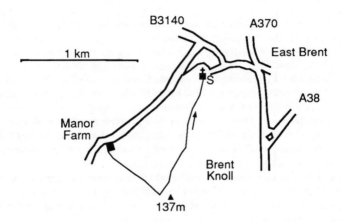

Take the path up the right side of the church, ignoring the signed path to the left –
which is the return route – and continuing to the back of the churchyard. Go right,
through a gate and cross the field ahead to reach Hill Lane. Go left along the lane to
reach Manor Farm, to the left. Go past the farm to reach a signed path to the left.
Follow this, going to the right of the buildings. Cross a field to a gate. Go through,
and follow the hedge on the right to the top of **Brent Knoll**.

   To return to East Brent, go to the northern end of the flat top, close to the flagpole,
and take the path which descends steeply to reach a stile. Go over and follow the path
which heads towards St Mary's church, going over several waymarked stiles. Close
to **East Brent** the path goes across the school playground to emerge at the church.

POINTS OF INTEREST:

Brent Knoll – For the casual visitor to Somerset, and particularly those that see it only from the M5, Brent Knoll is much more of a landmark than Glastonbury Tor, for although the latter can be seen – on a clear day – the Knoll towers above the road and the Sedgemoor service area. In fact, the Knoll is only 449 feet (137 metres) above sea level, but so low-lying are the Somerset Levels, and so flat, that it appears to be a real mountain. Anciently, when the sea covered the Levels the Knoll would have been an island. Indeed, in 1607 when the sea flooded the area for several months it was an island again.

The Romans called the Knoll *Mons Ranorum*, the Mount of Frogs, which was probably very apt before the Levels had been drained. Legend has it that the hill was created by the Devil when he threw a spade-full of earth over his shoulder as he was digging out Cheddar Gorge. An equally appealing legend has it that the hill was the scene of one of King Arthur's exploits, or, rather, one of his knights. The knight was Sir Ider, a young Welsh prince who was ordered by Arthur to fight three giants who were living on the hill and terrorising the locals. Ider rode off across the Levels, but when Arthur arrived several hours later he found the young knight dead, along with the three giants. Overcome by remorse Arthur gave the Knoll and the surrounding marshes to the church.

The Knoll was a fortress before the Romans came, the ramparts of an Iron Age hillfort being clearly seen, and was one long after they were gone when the Home Guard trenched it during the 1939–45 War. Happier times are remembered in the flagpole which is used as part of local celebrations. Bonfires are lit on the Knoll during times of Royal celebration.

East Brent – The village is famous for its Harvest Home festival on the third Thursday in August. The church, St Mary's, is worth visiting to see the delicate nave ceiling and the carved pew ends.

REFRESHMENTS:
The Knoll Inn, East Brent.

Walk 12   **COTHELSTONE HILL**   2m (3km)

Maps: OS Sheets Landranger 182; Pathfinder ST 03/13 and ST 23/33.

A short walk to a fine viewpoint.

Start: At 204327, the car park on Cothelstone Hill.

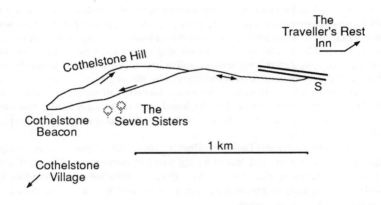

To reach the start it is best to drive west from North Petherton, taking the country lanes to Broomfield and Fyne Court. Now head for Merridge, reaching the junction of five roads on top of Buncombe Hill. Take the road westward, for Cothelstone and West Bagborough to reach the car park, which is on the left about 400 yards from the junction.

From the car park head west, going between wooden posts on to a wide path. After about 400 yards, at a junction of paths, bear left between gates and climb up to a prominent group of trees, the Seven Sisters, on the skyline. Walk past the trees to reach a cross path near a mound topped by the ruins of an old castle. This is **Cothelstone Beacon**.

Go right on the wide track and after about 250 yards go left at a fork on to a narrower path. Follow this path back to reach the outward path close to the two gates. From there return along the outward route back to the car park.

POINTS OF INTEREST:

Cothelstone Beacon – The Beacon is named for its ancient use as a signal fire hill. Recently, the 400th anniversary of the defeat of the Spanish Armada was celebrated with a beacon fire.

From the Beacon and, indeed, from most parts of the walk, the view is exceptional, including the Brendon Hills and Exmoor, Blackdown to the south, and the more immediate view of the Quantocks. The name Quantocks derives from the Saxon *cantocks*, stream headlands, a descriptive name for the geography of the hills which are actually a dissected plateau with streams draining down from the ridge watershed. In a charter of the 7th century West Saxon King, Centwine, the hills are termed *cantacudio*. The wooded combes are the home of red deer, the walker who visits the area in early morning having a good chance of seeing a small herd.

Cothelstone, the village at the south-western base of the hill, and for which the hill is named, is an interesting little place. Its church has two fine stained glass windows, one showing St Aldhelm, the other – in the Stawell Chapel – showing St Dunstan holding a pair of metal workers tongs. The chapel is named for the Stawell family, long time lords of the manor. One of the family, living in Cothelstone Manor at the time of Monmouth's rebellion, was so appalled at the Bloody Assizes that followed the battle of Sedgemoor that he refused to allow Judge Jefferies to stay when he arrived in the area. Outraged the Judge had two of Monmouth's men hanged from the battlements of the Manor's gatehouse.

REFRESHMENTS:

None on route, but the Traveller's Rest Inn is only about a mile away. To reach it go back to the five-road junction and take the road for Enmore.

Walks 13 & 14   THE RIVER FROME – ROUTES 2 AND 3   2m (3km) or 5m (8km)

Maps: OS Sheets Landranger 172; Pathfinder ST 67/77 and ST 68/68.

Shorter and longer walks in the delightful Frome Valley.

Start: At 646793, opposite the Chapel in Whiteshill.

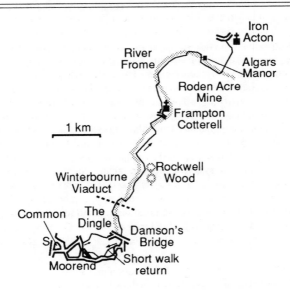

From the chapel cross the road and follow the right edge of the Common, heading towards the school. Cross Moorend Road and take Worrell's Lane, going down the right side of the school. At the oblique T-junction turn right into Mill Road. This quickly bridges the River Frome. Immediately over the bridge go left on a path signed for the Frome Valley Walkway. Follow the path with the river on your left hand until a footbridge is reached. Cross this and go right on a new path, with the river now on your right. When the path reaches The Dingle follow the road to its T-junction with Down Road. Go right here to quickly reach Damsons Bridge.

The shorter walk crosses the bridge and takes the next road on the right – Bury Hill – bearing right at a Y-junction with Cuckoo Lane. At the top of the hill, there is a stile on the right. Go over and take the path along the hedge to reach a stile. Go over – you are now back on Bury Hill – and turn left. About 200 yards further on take the signed footpath on the right towards Bury Hill Camp, a large hill fort. The camp is reached over a stile on the left: follow the path through it and down to a stile on to a road. Go left to reach a crossroads. Turn right on to Moorend Road and follow it back to the start. The final, steep, section is known locally as Jack and Jill Hill.

The longer route crosses Damsons Bridge and immediately turns left over a stile to reach a path along the river bank. The Walkway is now well-defined and signed, crossing the river just before the **Winterbourne Viaduct**, and recrossing it just after. Further on the path is hemmed in by the river – on the left – and Rockwell Wood – on the right. Do not cross the next bridge (Nightingale Bridge) but when another is reached (Parsonage Bridge) cross to the new housing estate on the outskirts of the old village of Frampton Cotterell. Stay close to the river to reach the village church.

The path reaches Church Road, emerging opposite the church. Go left, then right into Mill Lane. Go through the farm ahead, following signs for the Walkway to reach the river again, and continue with it on your right. The river is soon crossed, then recrossed on an iron bridge that once carried the tramway to the Roden Acre Mine.

Beyond the iron bridge the Walkway joins a lane and follows it over another bridge near Algars Manor. Go left and follow the river to yet another crossing point. Cross, and leave the Walkway by taking the path ahead through Chill Wood. Beyond the wood, cross a field to reach a railway embankment. This is an off-shoot line carrying stone from, and equipment to, the Tytherington quarries near Thornbury. The obvious crossing point is blocked, so go to the right to reach steps. Beyond the railway, walk to the top left corner of a field to reach a stile. Go over and turn left to reach **Iron Acton**, from where buses will take you back to the start of the walk.

POINTS OF INTEREST:
Winterbourne Viaduct – The 11-arched viaduct, a marvel of Victorian railway engineering, carries South Wales to London trains almost 100 feet over the Frome Valley.

Iron Acton – Although the village name is clearly linked with the mining of iron ore there have been no mines here since the time of the Romans. Technically the Roden Acre Mine, active in the second half of the 19th century, is in Frampton Cotterell. The mine's ore was taken by tram and railway to South Wales.

REFRESHMENTS:
The Star, Church Road, Frampton Cotterell.
The Rose and Crown, Iron Acton.

Walk 15   **BREAN DOWN**   2¹/₂m (4km)

Maps: OS Sheets Landranger 182; Pathfinder ST 25/35.

A surprising walk, with fine views.

Start: At 296586, the road end car park north of Brean.

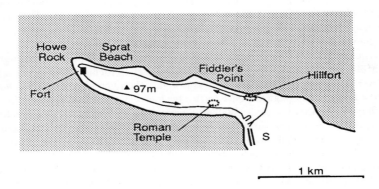

To reach the start drive north through Brean village on a road that runs at the beach's edge. The car park is where the road ends.

From the car park a lane, signed for the ferry which, in summer, plies across the mouth of the Axe to Weston-super-Mare, heads east. Take this lane, ignoring the steps to the left, and continuing to reach a path that also climbs towards **Brean Down**. Go up the path to reach an Information Board. Continue to the northern edge of the Down and turn along a path that stays close to the cliff's edge, going through the ramparts of an Iron Age hillfort and on to Fiddler's Point.

Continue westward on the path, ignoring all left turns. The path edges the cliffs above Sprat Beach to reach **Brean Fort**. After admiring the view cross Howe Rock, take the path that climbs to the ridge along the top of the Down, soon reaching the trig point Summit itself. From the trig point the path continues along the ridge, passing to the right of the indistinct remains of a Roman temple. When you are level with the car park turn towards it to reach the top of the steps ignored on the outward journey. Go down these to return to the start of the walk.

POINTS OF INTEREST:

Brean Down – The Down is owned by the National Trust, and is an SSSI (Site of Special Scientific Interest) for its wildflowers, and also as a nesting site for birds. The cliffs are the highest for many miles on the southern side of the Bristol Channel and therefore support a good collection of seabird species as well as several waders at the cliff base. The Down grasslands are home to skylarks, meadowlarks – especially pleasing in the early nesting season for their 'parachuting' mating flight – and stonechats. The cliffs on the southern side can be approached from the beach. They are both steep and unstable and should be avoided, even if there are rock climbers making them look straightforward. The beach is not pleasant at low tide, a broad band of thick mud being exposed by the retreating sea. The mud is silt from the River Severn and, despite the stories, is harmless. It is, however, sticky and unpleasant and difficult to remove.

Brean Fort – The fort was built in 1870 when there was a real fear of invasion by the armies of Napoleon III. It housed a number of 7 inch cannons pointing out to sea, the intention being to sink the army before it landed. The fort was also manned throughout the 1939–45 War.

Summit – Because of Brean Down's position – thrust out like a finger into the Bristol Channel – it offers a tremendous view. To the east are the Mendips, to the north and west the islands of Steep Holm and Flat Holm and the Welsh coast. To the south, to be exact the south-west, are the Quantocks and Exmoor.

REFRESHMENTS:

There are several cafés in Brean.

Walk 16   **HURLSTONE POINT**   2$\frac{1}{2}$m (4km)

Maps: OS Sheets Landranger 181; Pathfinder SS 84/94.

An easy walk to a fine viewpoint.

Start: At 898480, the car park in Bossington.

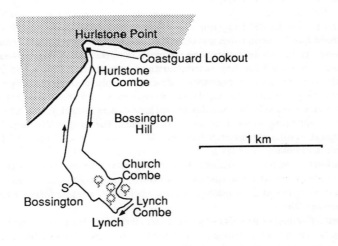

From the car park go over the footbridge and turn left along a path beside the stream. Soon the path bears right, away from the stream, going northwards towards the sea. Follow the path as it rises up to **Hurlstone Point**, reaching the Coastguard Lookout at the cliff edge.

Return along the outward path for about 100 yards, then go left at a path fork, leaving the outward route in favour of a path that heads inland at a higher level. The path goes across the bottom of Hurlstone Combe, which runs down from the northern flank of Bossington Hill, then climbs gently to reach a fine viewpoint at a spur of the hill. Beyond this the path curves gently around the hillside to reach a wood. Go along the edge of the wood to reach Church Combe. Do not continue up the combe – there is, in any case, no path – but go right, through a gate, into the wood, which has a good collection of the evergreen holm oaks.

Follow the path through the wood to reach a gate. Go through and continue to a junction of paths. Turn right on the path, signed for Bossington, which goes down wooded Lynch Combe. At the bottom of the combe bear right across a field, then turn left (at a signpost for Bossington) to reach a stream. Turn right on a path along the stream bank to reach the bridge crossed on the outward journey. Turn left over the bridge to return to **Bossington**.

POINTS OF INTEREST:

Hurlstone Point – Long ago a giant lived on Grabbist Hill near Dunster. One day he was challenged to a boulder throwing competition by the Devil. The two went to the cliff above Bossington and threw boulders along the coast. The two boulders now form the Whit Stones, off-shore to the west of Porlock. Realising he had been out-thrown the Devil tried to change the rules of the game. At that point the giant picked him up by the tail and hurled him out into the Channel. From that time on the cliff was known as Hurlstone Point. It is a nice story, but it seems that the name has only recently been changed from Huntstone Point.

From the Point the view is tremendous, taking in Porlock Bay and the coast beyond as far as Foreland Point, from which fall some of the highest cliffs in England.

There is a notice at the Point telling visitors that the cliffs are dangerous. The danger lies beyond the Coastguard Lookout, which should not be passed, except with extreme care.

Bossington – Bossington is one of the prettiest villages in Somerset, certainly a strong contender – with nearby Selworthy – for the title of the most delightful. The village lies within the National Trust's Holnicote Estate which ensures that it remains picturesque. At nearby Lynch, a hamlet to the south, the Somerset Farm Park has many old breeds of farm animals, while the agricultural museum is England's foremost private collection.

REFRESHMENTS:

The Bossington tea gardens are renowned for their cream teas. Those looking for something a little less rich can go into Porlock which caters for all tastes.

Walk 17   **TIMBERSCOMBE COMMON** $2^1/_2$m ($3^1/_2$km)

Maps: OS Sheets Landranger 181; Pathfinder SS 84/94.

A short walk on the Brendon Hills.

Start: At 969411, a clearing in the Croydon Hill Forest.

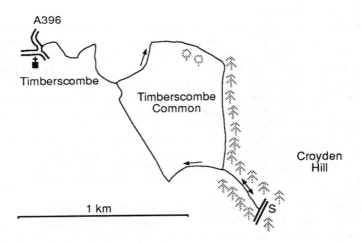

The start is to the side of the minor road which links the A396 near Dunster – go south from that village and turn off left after rounding Vinegar Hill – to Luxborough, at the heart of the Brendon Hills. This minor road goes around Croydon Hill, a hill now swamped by a Forestry Commission plantation. The clearing is close to the 'Steep Hill' warning sign.

From the clearing head north-west through a red waymarked gate and follow the forestry road downhill, going past a fire tower. The road reaches the edge of the plantation where another forestry road crosses. Go through the gate ahead into a field and follow the track through it to reach another gate. In this field there are fine views westward with Dunkery Beacon rising from the bulk of Exmoor.

Go through the gate ahead and turn right to go through another. Beyond this second gate a path contours around the edge of **Timberscombe Common**, going through another gate and then following the hedge. Continue until a small, red waymarked gate is reached. Go through and turn right, going gently uphill to reach a track near a copse of beautiful silver birch trees. The path to the left here, past the disused quarries, goes down to **Timberscombe** where refreshments are available.

Follow the track north-east, bearing left along the field edge when it is reached, to reach a gate with a yellow waymarker. Go right here, and follow the power lines across the field, staying below a small wood and continuing to reach the Forestry Commission plantation again. Go through another yellow waymarked gate and turn right through a gap in a bank to reach the forest edge track crossed earlier in the walk. Walk down this track until the outward route is reached. Turn left along the outward forestry road to return to the start.

POINTS OF INTEREST:

Timberscombe Common – The Brendon Hills are an eastern outlier of Exmoor, separated from the main moor by the valleys of the Avill and Quarme rivers. In form they are a single east-west running, broad ridge cut into by a complex network of combes. That would seem to make them geographically more similar to the Quantocks, to the east, but despite there being almost no high moor left now the Brendons are genuinely part of Exmoor and are included in the Exmoor National Park.

The view from this walk around Timberscombe Common is dominated by Dunkery Beacon, but in the section where the walk heads north, after Timberscombe, the view downhill, to the Avill valley, is superb.

Timberscombe – The village is delightfully positioned in the wooded valley of a tributary of the Avill, but suffers a little from having the A396 running through its western edge, taking holiday traffic down to Dunster and the coast. Perhaps this is only fair in view of the village's prosperous past as a coach stop. The Rock Inn is an old coaching inn. The attractive church is largely 15th century and is dedicated, unusually, to St Petroc. The tower was rebuilt in the 17th century, the little spire having been added at the time of Queen Anne.

REFRESHMENTS:

None on route, but if the detour to Timberscombe is taken the Rock Inn can be visited.

Walks 18 & 19 THE WELLOW BROOK 2½m (4km) or 5m (8km)

Maps: OS Sheets Landranber 172; Pathfinder ST 65/75 and ST 66/76.

Two fine walks around the Wellow Brook south of Bath.

Start: At 741583, the village square, Wellow.

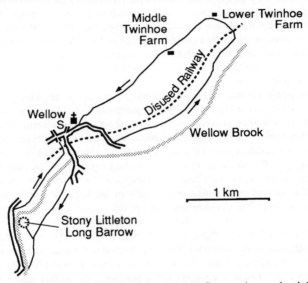

From the square walk towards the church, but take the first turning on the right. Follow the road across the bridge over the Wellow Brook and on to a Y-junction. Bear right and after about 100 yards take the signed bridlepath on the right. After about 800 yards the bridlepath ends at a gate: follow the path beyond across a field. The **Stoney Littleton** long barrow can soon be seen to the right: do not cross to it as you will be trespassing. Instead, continue until a signed path leading back to the tumulus is reached.

After visiting the long barrow return to the main path, turning right on to it and going downhill to reach a footbridge over the Wellow Brook. Cross the bridge and turn right on a road which is heading back to Wellow. After 800 yards go over the stile (or through the gate) on the right into a field. The path through this field and the following ones stays close to the bank of the Wellow Brook, offering a delightful stretch of walking. Where the brook goes right, and the path fades, go over a stile in the hedge to the left to reach a clearer path. Follow this path to where it emerges between cottages in Wellow and from there follow the outward route back to the start.

To continue the walk, turn right to go past the church, following the road under bridge that once carried the **Somerset and Dorset Railway**. About 400 yards beyond the bridge – and about 100 yards beyond the Trekking Centre – go left on a curious fenced bank. Go through a gate and follow a path which runs parallel to the old railway, both path and railway contouring around the hillside. Eventually a hedge is reached. Go left of it and uphill to reach Hankly Wood. Go through the wood, exiting downhill and soon reaching a once gated gap. Go through and turn left under a railway bridge. Go through a gate and climb steeply up a stony track. Near Lower Twinhoe Farm there is a T-junction of tracks: turn left up the green lane, crossing two fields to reach Middle Twinhoe.

At Middle Twinhoe, pass a stable on the left and go through a gate to reach the farm drive. After 20 yards go left through a gate and climb a field to a stile. Cross the field ahead close to the right fence and go through a gate. Continue to climb to the top of the ridge ahead. Soon, go through a gate on to a road. Go left, but as the road turns right, continue ahead, following the left hedge of a field. Wellow is now in sight ahead. Stay with the hedge, going over three stiles to reach the valley bottom. Cross marshy ground to reach a grass lane. Now go over a stile on the right and cross a field to the churchyard of St Julian's church, Wellow. Go left over a stile and along the wall to reach a lane. Turn right to reach the churchyard and the start of the walk.

POINTS OF INTEREST:
Stoney Littleton Long Barrow - The long barrow is a burial chamber constructed by folk of the Neolithic (New Stone) Age. The barrow was probably built about 4,500 years ago. The burial chamber consists of large flat stones which form a box, reached by a passage that is also formed of flat stones. The whole was then earthed over to form the barrow, which is 100 feet long. The entrance is set within a pair of drystone wall 'horns', the walling technique being identical to that still in use in Britain.

Somerset and Dorset Railway – The railway was constructed in 1862 and is remembered for its picturesque ride. It was closed by Dr Beeching in 1966.

REFRESHMENTS:
The Fox and Badger, Wellow.

SAND POINT   3m (5km)

Maps: OS Sheets Landranger 182; Pathfinder ST 26/36.

A surprisingly beautiful section of coastline.

Start: At 330659, the road end, National Trust, car park north of Weston-super-Mare.

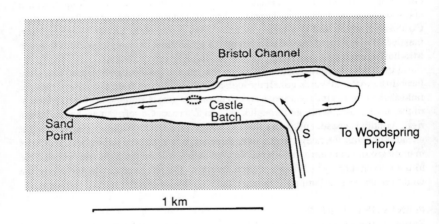

To find the start from Weston just follow the seafront road northward, passing the Grand Pier, to your left, then the Winter Gardens, to the right. Now pass the Knightstone/Marine Lake complex on the left and round the headland to reach Burnbeck Pier. Ahead now the road hugs a terrace at the base of Worlebury Hill to reach the more gentle Sand Bay. Drive along the back of the beach to reach the car park.

Leave the car park and go up the steps behind the toilets to reach a path. Follow the path to where it is divided by an old wall. Take the path to the left of the wall to reach open ground. The wedge of high land that forms Middle Hope is not high, the trig point – set on **Castle Batch** – stands at 157 feet (48 metres), but is certainly an impressive viewpoint, especially from **Sand Point**, the extreme westerly point. The footpath heads directly for the Point. From it, double back and take the lower path which stays close to the northern edge of Middle Hope. This is Swallow Cliff: children should be watched carefully here as the cliff edge is unfenced and the fall uninviting.

The path descends to reach a gate below Castle Batch. Go through to reach open land again, now just a few feet above the beach. Continue to reach a bay of pebbles and from it take the path that climbs back up on to Middle Hope to reach a wall. Cross this by ladder stile and turn right along the wall. To the left now **Woodspring Priory** can be seen. When steps are reached on the left, take them to arrive back at the car park.

POINTS OF INTEREST:

Castle Batch – The castle is all that remains of a motte and bailey fortress, the Normans then having realised the defensive potential of the site.

Sand Point – It is likely that Middle Hope was once an island standing a few hundred yards off-shore and that it was joined to the mainland when silt from the River Severn raised the local level of the seabed. Its obvious defensive position was noted in earliest times, there being evidence of both Celtic and Roman camps. During the 1939–45 War, Middle Hope was used as a testing ground for secret weapons.

From Sand Point the walker will be able to see not only Burnbeck Pier and Worlebury Hill, but Steep Holm and the Welsh coast around Cardiff.

Woodspring Priory – The Priory was founded for an Augustinian Order by the Normans in the 13th century, though what is now seen dates from the 15th century. After the dissolution of the monastries by Henry VIII the Priory was put to a variety of uses as farm outbuilding, golf club and curious ruin. It is now being restored.

REFRESHMENTS:

None on route, but easily obtainable in nearby Weston-super-Mare.

Walk 21   VELVET BOTTOM   3m (5km)

Maps: OS Sheets Landranger 182, Pathfinder ST 45/55.
Simply the best short walk on Mendip.
Start: At 504556, the car park at Blackmoor.

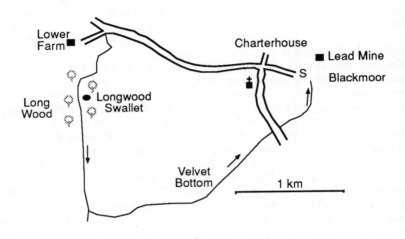

To reach the start, take the B3134 road up Burrington Combe, and turn first left, past Paywell Farm, on the minor road for Charterhouse and Priddy. Where a road turns off right for Shipham after about 1 mile, go left down a narrow lane beside the outdoor centre – with a prominent observatory dome in its grounds – to reach a car park.

From the car park walk back up the access road to the junction. Go straight across, passing **Charterhouse** church, to the left, and take the road for Shipham. Walk past Manor Farm to reach the edge of Long Wood, to the left. As the wood ends, a lane to the left leads down to Lower Farm. Take this lane, but go left almost immediately on a path through **Long Wood**. The path passes the entrance to Longwood Swallet and continues through the wood, which forms the Long Wood Nature Reserve. Ignore turnings off the main path, continuing along it until it exits the wood to reach a path junction. Turn right here on to the West Mendip Way (*see* Note to Walk 66). Go over a stile, beyond which, to the left, there is an old iron water pump dated 1884, and walk for another 200 yards to reach a stone stile on the left. Go over the stile to reach the path through **Velvet Bottom**. Follow the path to a road. Cross and continue along the road to reach the **Blackmoor** car park.

POINTS OF INTEREST:

Charterhouse – In 1184 St Bruno, appalled by what he saw as the ungodliness of French monastries, founded a new type of monastic house at Great Charterhouse in Provence. In Bruno's house the monks lived a solitary life. Each had his own cell and garden, coming together with his fellow monks only in church. When St Bruno's ideas came to Britain, the houses were called priories, although they were also frequently called charterhouses, a name derived from the first house in Provence. The monks that lived in the Priory were called Carthusians. In Britain one of the first Carthusian houses was Witham Priory, founded in the 12th century. The Witham monks were granted the rights to the Mendip lead mining area that lay close to a scatter of houses nestling below the highest ground. In time that scattered hamlet became known as Charterhouse after its owners. When the Prior of Witham visited the area he stayed in a house which is believed to have stood where Manor Farm, an excellent 17th century house, now stands.

Long Wood – The name of the wood is believed to be Saxon, this fine broadleaf wood therefore having a remarkable pedigree. The Nature Reserve was set up to protect the eco-system of the wood where trees include spindle, elder and dogwood as well as the more usual oak, beech, hazel and blackthorn. The prominent cave entrance on the walk, a locked manhole, leads to Longwood Swallet, one of the most challenging of the Mendip caves.

Velvet Bottom – The delightfully named Velvet Bottom is a dry valley, famous for its wildflowers, and also a favourite with adders.

Blackmoor – The Romans certainly mined the area around the car park, the largest Roman lead pig ever found in Britain – weighing 100 kgs (220 lbs) – having been discovered here. Local legend has it that the mines were in operation earlier, and that Joseph of Aramathea came to Somerset in order to buy Charterhouse lead.

To the north of the car park are the extensive remains of more recent mining, with heaps of vitreous slag, the remains of horizontal flues – where lead dust was collected from the walls after it had dropped out of furnace smoke – and other ruins. The area is not safe for small children to roam at will, but is fascinating.

REFRESHMENTS:

None on route, but available in nearby Shipham, or in Burrington Combe.

Walk 22   **KING'S SEDGEMOOR**   3m (5km)

Maps: OS Sheets Landranger 182; Pathfinder ST 33/33.

A walk in the shadow of history.

Start: At 352348, St Mary's Church, Westonzoyland.

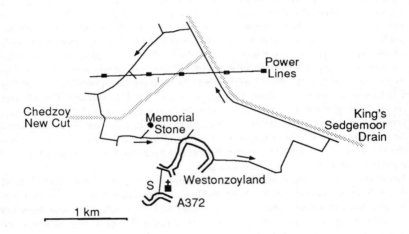

Go north along Church Lane – which lies to the west of the church. Where the road goes right continue ahead on a footpath to reach Monmouth Road. Go right, along this, bearing left with it to reach Bussex Farm. Here the road goes sharply left: stay with it as it makes a long right bend. Now turn left along a lane which is a footpath despite the sign. Go through a gate and turn left just beyond an old RAF building. Go diagonally right across a field to reach another gate. Go through and immediately left through another gate. Go across a field to reach a gate on to a track. Go right along the track for 500 yards, ignoring a track to the right, to reach a footpath to the left which heads for a footbridge over **King's Sedgemoor Drain**. Do not go over the bridge: instead, turn left along the Drain bank. Follow the bank for $^{3}/_{4}$ mile (1,200 metres), going over several stiles, to where it turns half-right.

    Continue along the Drain for a further 600 yards to reach a bridge over Chedzoy

New Cut, a new drainage rhine (pronounced *rheen*) cut into the Drain. About halfway between the turn and the new cut the route goes under power lines. The sphere on the lines are to warn birds of their presence: this is to protect both the birds and the lines. Continue along the Drain for a further 400 yards to reach a track to the left which heads away from the Drain. Follow this track to its junction with another, cross, track. Go left on this new track. Go under the power lines, and continue for another 400 yards to reach a path to the left, its start marked by hedges.

Follow the path across a field to reach a bridge over Chedzoy New Cut. Cross the bridge, go left for 20 yards, then turn right down the side of a hedge. At the bottom, go left through a gate and cross to another. Go through this gate on to a lane. Go left, following the lane around a sharp corner. About 250 yards beyond the corner a signed turn to the left leads to the **battlefield memorial**. Return to the lane and turn left, i.e. continue as you were before the detour to the memorial. Continue to reach a road and turn right to retrace the outward route for the last few steps through **Westonzoyland**.

POINTS OF INTEREST:

King's Sedgemoor Drain – The Drain was cut in the last years of the 18th century to ease flooding on the Levels.

Battlefield Memorial – In 1685, when Charles II died, the throne was claimed by his brother, James II. At the time of Charles' death his eldest, but illegitimate, son – also called James, and made Duke of Monmouth by his father – was in Holland. Sensing a dislike of his uncle, Monmouth landed at Lyme Regis, in Dorset, in order to raise an army for a march on Mondon. Within a fortnight Monmouth had raised an army of 3,500 men – though they were badly armed and untrained – and had won a small battle near Bath, where 80 men of the Royal army were killed. But rain dampened Monmouth's army's spirits and they retreated to Bridgwater. A Royal army marched to Westonzoyland where it stayed overnight on 5–6 July. Hoping for a surprise attack Monmouth lead his men across Sedgemoor towards the village, but his men became hopelessly lost in the marshes. Dawn on 6th July found them tired and weary, and in the last battle fought on English soil they were utterly defeated. Over 2,000 men were killed, hundreds more in the Bloody Assizes that followed.

Westonzoyland – The church of St Mary's, a fine one, was used as a temporary prison after the battle, 500 men being herded into it, several of them dying of their wounds.

REFRESHMENTS:

The Sedgemoor Inn, Westonzoyland.

Walk 23   **NORTH WOOTTON**   3m (5km)

Maps: OS Sheets Landranger 183; Pathfinder ST 44/54.

A walk dominated by views of Glastonbury Tor.

Start: At 564418, the church in North Wootton.

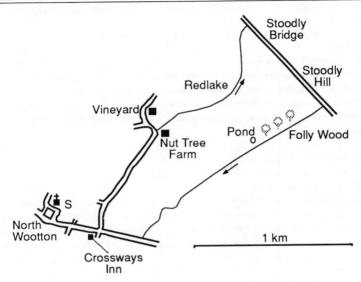

Go along the lane in front of the church, bearing right after the Redlake stream has been crossed to reach a T-junction. Go left to reach the Crossways Inn, turning left at the cross-roads beside it. Follow this road for 800 yards to where it bends sharply left. If the road is followed here, and a turn to the right is taken at the next junction, **North Wootton Vineyards** can be visited.

The walk does not follow the road, going straight on along the farm lane to Nut Tree Farm. Go between farm buildings on the clear track across farmland above the shallow valley of the Redlake stream. Eventually, the track bears left and heads towards the stream, reaching a road near Stoodly Bridge, which crosses it. Go right, along the road which climbs steeply up Stoodly Hill. The only compensation for the climb is that pauses for breath allow an inspection of Warminster Sleight, the domed hill to the north.

46

At the top of Stoodly Hill, before a Y-junction is reached, a bridlepath leads off to the right, reaching, and following, the southern edge of **Folly Wood**. Ignore all side paths to reach a gate beside a small pond. Go across two fields following the field edges, then bear half-left in the third to reach a stile among trees. Go over the stile and follow the lane beyond downhill to reach a road. Go right, along the road, to reach the cross-roads at the aptly named Crossways Inn. From there reverse the outward route to the church.

POINTS OF INTEREST:

North Wooton Vineyards – Forsaking the usual Somerset beverage of cider, the villages of North Wooton and Pilton have now become the centre of the Somerset wine-making industry. The Manor House in Pilton offers visitors the chance to understand the mysteries of the process, as do the North Wooton Vineyards, where the vines and the buildings are open to the public from Monday to Saturday. Wine can also be purchased.

Folly Wood – On the route close to this delightful wood the view is dominated by Glastonbury Tor, rising from the Somerset Levels.

REFRESHMENTS:

The Crossways Inn, North Wootton.

The inn is famous for its excellent restaurant food, though walkers wanting to try the menu may find they need to book in advance.

Walk 24   **St Catherine's**   3m (5km)

Maps: OS Sheets Landranger 172; Pathfinder ST 66/76 and ST 67/77.

A delightful short walk from an interesting old building.

Start: At 778703, St Catherine's Court.

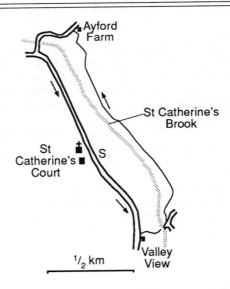

The Court stands in an almost secret valley which is reached by a narrow, and occasionally difficult, lane which leaves the A46 about 1m (1½km) south of Cold Ashton, and emerges on to the A4 a couple of hundred yards west of Batheaston. The valley can also be reached by lanes from Marshfield. Once in the valley the Court is obvious, and there is a small parking area across from it.

From the Court, head south down the valley – that is, away from Cold Ashton and towards Batheaston. The lane has a beautiful row of trees. Pass Lodge and Orchard Farms and then watch on the left for a signed path that leads downhill. The Mead Tea Gardens, the route's only possibility for refreshment, are a little further on: if you reach them, indeed if you reach the aptly named Valley View, you have gone too far!

Go down the path and cross St Catherine's Brook by footbridge to reach a lane that links the houses here to a road. Close to the junction there is a stile – waymarked with a yellow arrow. Similar arrows can be seen all along the route, which now follows the Brook. Cross a field, then take a rough track towards some old buildings. Do not walk to them: instead, go left into a field and cross it to reach a gate. Cross the next field to a stile. Go over and cross the field beyond to reach another stile. You will now be somewhat closer to the Brook. Its waters, and the shelter of the valley, mean the vegetation is very lush, and in wet weather can make the walk a damp outing.

Go to the right of a small copse to reach a track that reaches a road close to Ayford Farm. Go left, recross the Brook and walk up to a T-junction. Go left and follow the road back to reach **St Catherine's Court**.

POINTS OF INTEREST:

St Catherine's Court – The Court began life as part of a Benedictine monastery, and the remains of the monks' fish ponds can still be seen. When Henry VIII dissolved the monasteries he gave the house to his tailor John Malte. This remarkable act of generosity was not quite what it seemed – the gift required Malte to adopt Ethelreda, Henry's illegitimate daughter who was becoming an embarassment at Court. Around this time St Catherine's was remodelled, the beautiful Tudor mansion we now see being created.

The Court is private, but the church beside it can be visited. It was built for the Benedictines in the 13th century, though it has later additions. The fine stained glass window depicting the Crucifixion is 15th century.

From the Court the excellent 19th century Ashwicke Grange can be seen on the skyline on the far side of the valley.

REFRESHMENTS:
The Mead Tea Gardens, St Catherine's.

Walk 25   GLASTONBURY   3¹/₂m (5¹/₂km)

Maps: OS Sheets Landranger 182; Pathfinder ST 43/53.

A walk that includes both Abbey and Tor.

Start: At 498389, the Market Cross in Glastonbury.

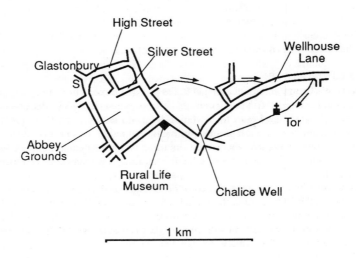

From the Market Cross go eastward up High Street. After about 200 yards, opposite St John the Baptist church, go right up a narrow lane. Turn left into Silver Street and walk to its end. Turn right into Lambrook Street – which soon becomes Chilkwell Street – to reach Abbey House. There, cross the road and go up Dod Lane. Where the lane goes right, walk ahead, passing Chalice School and reaching a stile. Go over, and follow the path ahead over a small hill to reach a gate on to a lane.

Walk along the lane to where it goes sharply left. There go straight ahead on a path, going over a stile and crossing a field to reach another. Go over this stile and go downhill, half-right, to reach a stile on to Wellhouse Lane. Go over the stile and turn left along the lane. Walk along the lane until a stile and signed (National Trust) path is reached on the right. Follow this path to the top of **Glastonbury Tor**.

From the chapel on top of the Tor take the clear path that descends southwestwards, crossing several stiles to reach Wellhouse Lane. Turn left along the lane and turn immediately right into Chilkwell Street. Go first right up a lane to reach **Chalice Well**. Return to Chilkwell Street – turning right along it – and follow it until a left turn into Bere Street can be made. Walk past the **Rural Life Museum**, to the left, and continue to the cross-roads at the bottom of Bere Street. Go right into Fisher's Hill and follow it back to the start, passing the entrance to **Glastonbury Abbey** to the right.

POINTS OF INTEREST:

Glastonbury Tor – The manner in which the conical Tor dominates the local Somerset Levels has made it inevitable that it would be the centre of attraction. The facts about the Tor are easily established: a chapel existed on the top as early as the 12th century, being destroyed by an earthquake in 1275. The present chapel, to St Michael, was built in the 14th century, but has been ruinous for many years. In complete contrast, the Tor was the site of a gallows in medieval times, Abbot Whiting of Glastonbury being hanged there in 1539 after the dissolution of the Abbey.

More interesting to most visitors are the legends of Glastonbury, and its links with Earth Magic. The terraces around the Tor are said to map out a Cretan maze, which, if followed, lead to the Underworld. Another legend has it that the area surrounding the Tor has the signs of the Zodiac imprinted on its geography.

Chalice Well – The well is actually a natural spring which was Glastonbury's water supply until just a century ago. The name, however is from an old legend. This has it that Joseph of Aramathea visited Glastonbury as a merchant. On one visit, Joseph is said to have brought with him the Holy Grail, the chalice used at the Last Supper, and to have buried it beneath the spring. To support the legend the spring water is tinged with red, though this is more likely to be haematite, iron ore, staining.

Rural Life Museum – The museum is housed in the 14th century Abbey Barn and has exhibits on 19th and early 20th century domestic and agricultural life.

Glastonbury Abbey – Within the Abbey grounds is the Holy Thorn which flowers at Christmas. Legend has it that it grew from the staff of Joseph of Aramathea which he thrust into the ground. Later, King Arthur's grave was reputedly discovered at the Abbey, though most scholars believe that the tombstone – which has since disappeared – was a hoax by the monks to drum up interest in the Abbey which was suffering financial difficulties. The remains of the Abbey are fascinating, and the grounds very peaceful.

REFRESHMENTS:
Every taste is catered for in Glastonbury.

Walk 26   **SELWORTHY BEACON** $3^1/_2$m (6km)

Maps: OS Sheets Landranger 181; Pathfinder SS 84/94.

A walk that starts at Somerset's most famous village.

Start: At 919467, the car park in Selworthy.

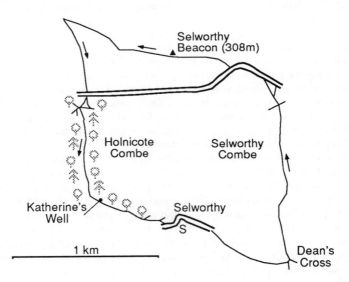

Go out of the car park and turn right along the road, following it to the staggered junction at Dean's Cross. Go left into Dean's Lane and follow it uphill to a gate. Go through and continue uphill, looking down left to see Selworthy Combe. The hut visible here is Lady Acland's Hut, built in 1870 for Gertrude, the wife of Sir Charles Acland who owned a great deal of land locally, much of which was given, most generously, to the National Trust.

Continue along the track to a junction. Go over and continue to reach another junction. Bear left here to reach a road. Go left for about 150 yards to reach a track on the right that leads to the trig point summit of **Selworthy Beacon**.

From the summit take the rough track westward to join the Somerset and North Devon Coastal Path. Follow the Path to its junction with a broad track. Turn left along this track, bearing left at a fork, down to a road. Cross and go around a vehicle barrier on to a track. Bear right at a junction soon after to reach a junction of several paths. Turn left here, and almost immediately left again on to a path that leads south down Holnicote Combe. Go through a gate and continue to reach a path junction. Go over and continue to another junction. There turn left on to a path. At the bend ahead go through a gap in the fence to the right to reach **Katherine's Well**. The path ahead has woodland on its left and farmland on its right: stay on it until it meets a broader path. Turn right here, and right again a little further on to reach **Selworthy** at the village green. Turn left past the National Trust shop to reach the church, to the left, and the car park, to the right.

POINTS OF INTEREST:

Selworthy Beacon – The summit here is at 1,010 feet (308 metres) and offers a wonderful panorama along the coast to Foreland Point, to the west, and back towards Minehead. Across the Channel, on clear days, the Gower Peninsula is visible. The beacon is named for its old use as a signal hill. A fire was lit here to warn of the sighting of the Spanish Armada. To the east of the Beacon the flank of the hill is dotted with tumuli, Bronze Age burial mounds.

Katherine's Well – This is an old Holy Well, probably dating from Celtic times when such springs were thought to have healing, or other magical, powers.

Selworthy – There are many who claim that Selworthy, with its little group of thatched cottages and its delightful church, is the prettiest village in England, let alone in Somerset. It has stiff competition for that title, but is really picturesque. The church tower is 14th century, but the best part is the south aisle, a gem of late 15th century architecture. Inside, there are three memorials to members of the Acland family by the sculpter Sir Francis Chantry.

REFRESHMENTS:

There is a seasonal tea shop in Selworthy. For more substantial, or pub, meals the walker must go to Porlock, to the west, or Minehead, to the east.

Walk 27   **BARWICK PARK**   3$\frac{1}{2}$m (5$\frac{1}{2}$km)

Maps: OS Sheets Landranger 183 & 194; Pathfinder ST 41/51.

A fine park on the Somerset-Dorset border.

Start: The Old Station car park, Yeovil.

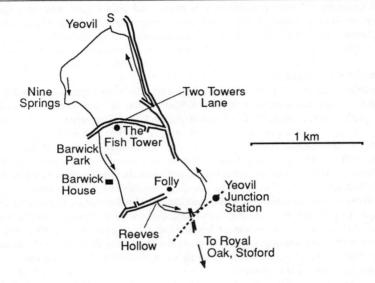

The car park is in the southern part of the town, just off the A30.

Leave the car park along the bed of the old track, heading south-west. Bear right at a play area and cross a bridge. Just beyond, turn left over a small bridge and walk up to the bottom of some steps. Go up the steps and turn left at the top, bearing left in front of a garage. Now follow the path beside **Nine Springs**, ignoring all side turnings, to reach a waterfall. Cross the stream above the waterfall and go left on a path beside a fence to reach a kissing gate on the right (beyond the ordinary gate). Go through and diagonally uphill across a field to reach another kissing gate. Go through and walk along the hedge to the left to reach yet another kissing gate, this one on to a road (Two Tower Lane).

Cross the road to a stile. Go over on a path signed for Barwick. Cross two fields, using stiles to cross between them, to reach the drive to **Barwick House**. Go left along

54

the drive to reach a road. Turn left and follow the road for 300 yards into Reeves Hollow to reach a gate, to the right. Go through to a path signed for Yeovil Junction. Walk down to an old mill and, just beyond, leave the main path to go down to a footbridge over a stream. Go up the bank ahead and over a stile in a small paddock. Cross to another stile and go over it on to a path behind some houses. Follow this to a road. Cross the road close to the railway bridge and walk up towards the station. Before the station is reached go left through a kissing gate on to a track. Go left off of this to reach the River Yeo and follow it to reach a bridge among trees.

Cross the bridge and go up steps. Turn half-left and cross a field to a stile on to a road. Turn right and follow the road past a turning to the **Coker villages** and its junction with Two Tower Lane. About 250 yards beyond this junction bear left on a metalled lane, leaving this soon after in favour of a path to the right signed for Yeovil Old Station. Follow this path through the delightful Newton Copse to reach a stile. Go over and turn left to reach a stile on to a bridge back to the car park.

POINTS OF INTEREST:

Nine Springs – This section of parkland was landscaped in the 18th century, the nine springs of the name being re-routed to create several waterfalls, one of which is passed by the walk.

Barwick House – In the early 18th century George Messiter, appalled by the misery caused by the failure of the local glove-making trade, used unemployed men to build four follies in the park surrounding Barwick House. One of these, the Fish Tower, is glimpsed on the walk. The most famous, Jack the Treacle Eater, is a little further along Reeves Hollow from where the walk turns south from it. The curious name derives from a story that Messiter sent employees on trips to London, by foot, with only a large amount of treacle as food for the trip. The Reeves Hollow folly was said to represent a foot sore, and mouth sore, walker.

Coker villages – There are three villages, North, West and East, the latter being the most famous as the poet T S Eliot is buried in its churchyard.

REFRESHMENTS:

None on route, but the Royal Oak on The Green in Staford is only about 600 yards south of Yeovil Junction Station, and there are many possibilities in Yeovil.

Walks 28 & 29 **BURRINGTON COMBE** 4m (6¹/₂km) or 8m (13km)
Maps: OS Sheets Landranger 182; Pathfinder ST 45/55.
The best walking on the northern Mendips.
Start: At 476588, the car park across from the Rock of Ages.

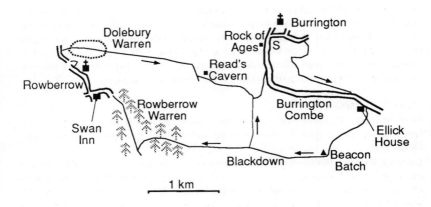

From the car park go right, down the Burrington Combe road and turn right after the Garden Centre. Go up the road, ignoring a road to the left. At the crest of the hill there is a path to the right, through trees. Take this. The path soon reaches a wood and follows its edge. Where another path goes off to the right take it, going through bracken to reach a T-junction with a wide grassy ride. Go right and uphill to an outcrop of rocks. Go left on another grassy ride which heads towards the Combe edge, but then bears left to run parallel with it. This ride reaches a lay-by/car park at the top of the Combe. Cross and go left along the road, passing Ellick House to the right. Turn right up the side of the house on a path which soon reaches a grassy ride through the bracken.

There are two possible routes now: the first climbs directly to the ridge above, turning right along it to reach the trig point on Beacon Batch, at 1,065 feet (325 metres) the highest point on Mendip. The second goes half-right, climbing to the

56

ridge more or less directly at the trig point. From the trig point take the wide grassy ride along the wide ridge, heading towards the distant forest. After $^3/_4$ mile, a narrow ride is reached which heads off down the hillside towards Burrington Combe – if you reach an extremely wide ride (some 150 yards wide) you have gone too far!

The shorter route takes this path which heads down the valley of the West Twin Brook. The gradient eases slightly, and at that point a narrow path branches off right. Follow the path, which quickly finds its way into shrubs and trees. The path becomes very stony: it actually goes along the bed of the Brook and after heavy rain can be a little difficult, though drier alternatives have been forged through the undergrowth. The path passes the entrances to **Goatchurch Cavern** and Sidcot Swallet before reaching the Burrington Combe road. Go left along the footpath to the side of the road, passing Aveline's Hole before reaching the **Rock of Ages**.

The longer route does not turn down the grassy ride but crosses the wide ride to reach a path into the conifer plantation of Rowberrow Warren. Keep on the main path through the forest, ignoring all side turnings. Eventually the path loses height rapidly and swings around to the left to join a path beside a stream. Turn right along this path following it up to join a lane. Follow the lane to the hamlet of Rowberrow. At a T-junction, turn right past the Swan Inn and continue past the church. About 150 yards further on take a path to the right which runs beside a fence. Follow it uphill to reach a cross path. Turn left along the path to a gate. Go along the lane beyond to reach a house on the right. Take the path up its left side to reach **Dolesbury Warren**. Go across the hillfort on the well-worn path that reaches a stile on to a track. Go right, downhill, to reach a path along the northern edge of Rowberrow Warren. Go left along this path to emerge on the wide grassy ride crossed earlier. Continue ahead to reach the narrow ride of the shorter route close to where the path heads down to West Twin Brook. Now follow the shorter route back to the start.

POINTS OF INTEREST:
Goatchurch Cavern – The cave is one of many in the Mendip limestone. They are formed by rainwater, which is slightly acidic, eating away the limestone at natural points of weakness.
Rock of Ages – As the plaque on the cliff notes, the obvious cleft in the rock is where the Rev Toplady sheltered from a storm and was inspired to write the famous hymn.
Dolebury Warren – The hillfort is an Iron Age camp covering almost 20 acres.

REFRESHMENTS:
The Burrington Combe Restaurant and café.
The Swan Inn, Rowberrow.

Walk 30   **MILBORNE PORT**   4m (6½km)

Maps: OS Sheets Landranger 183; Pathfinder ST 61/71.
A Somerset walk just a couple of miles from Dorset's Sherborne.
Start: At 678191, the Village Hall car park, Milborne Port.

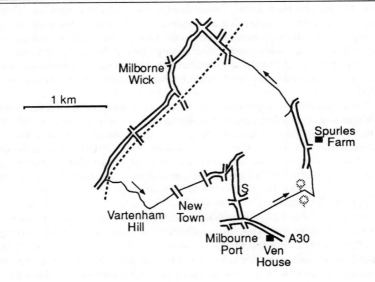

Walk back to the main village road, North Street, and turn left along it to reach the main A30 road which bisects the lower half of **Milborne Port**. Go left along the A30, then left again up East Street. Where the road goes sharp left go right to reach two footpaths. Take the enclosed path to the right signed for Crendle Hill and follow it to a stile. Cross this and go over three fields, using stiles to go between them, to reach a wood: on the right of this section **Ven House** can be seen. Go through a gate into the wood and follow a path upwards to reach a gate. Go through and left on to an enclosed path. Follow this to the stile at its end. Go over and cross the field beyond to reach a stile on to a road. Go right and walk past the lane to Spurles Farm.

Where the road goes sharp right, turn back left on to a track to reach, shortly, a stile on the right. Go over this on to a path through a wood. When the path forks go left and walk to a stile. Go over and cross the field beyond to a stile on to a road. Turn right and follow the road under a railway bridge and past a right turn to reach a staggered junction. Turn left here and follow the road to the hamlet of Milborne Wick. At the cross-roads in the hamlet go left past an old mill to reach Browns Farm, to the left.

Turn right opposite the farm and walk to a cross-roads. Go over and walk along the road for another 700 yards to reach a railway bridge on the left. At this point the walker has reached the Somerset-Dorset border, but does not venture into Dorset, turning left over the bridge to reach a stile into a field. Follow the hedge on the right to a stile. Go over and keep right to reach a stile in the field corner. Go over and walk up the elegantly named Vartenham Hill, staying close to the left-hand hedge. Stay with the hedge around a left bend and go through the gate ahead. Cross two fields to reach a gate on to an enclosed path that goes between the houses of **New Town** to reach a road.

Cross the road to reach a track to the rear of some houses and follow it to Wick Road. Cross to reach Court Lane and follow this downhill to a footbridge. Go over and turn left, then bear right to a road. Walk along the road to reach steps, to the right, that lead up to a kissing gate. Cross a field to another kissing gate and cross the road beyond to reach an alley. Go up this to reach the village hall and take the last few steps of an enjoyable walk back to the car park.

POINTS OF INTEREST:

Milborne Port – The village was important in Saxon times, being home to one of the Royal mints. St John's Church has some remaining Saxon features, though it was largely rebuilt in Norman times.

Ven House – This elegant house was built in the late 17th century, the parkland surrounding it having been landscaped and an excellent avenue of trees planted along the house drive. The remaining trees of this avenue can still be seen.

New Town – This odd addition to the village was built by the local Member of Parliament when his majority was in danger.

REFRESHMENTS:
The King's Head, High Street, Milborne Port.

Walk 31   **ALFRED'S TOWER**   4m (6¹/₂km)

Maps: OS Sheets Landranger 183; Pathfinder ST 63/73.

From an historical monument into an ancient wood.

Start: At 745351, the car park at Alfred's Tower.

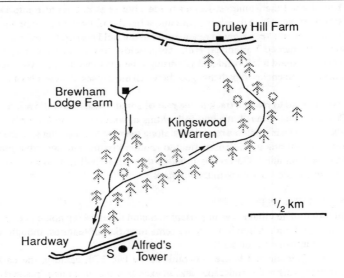

The car park is reached by going north from Wincanton on the B3081 towards Bruton. Turn right at Redlynch on to a minor road, and follow it for 3¹/₂ miles (5¹/₂km) to reach Alfred's Tower, to the right of the road.

From the car park go back to the road – the **Hardway** – and turn left, back the way you have come if you have followed the instructions above. After 200 yards go right on a forest track signed for Druley Hill and **Kingswood Warren**. Follow this track for 800 yards to a fork. Take the right fork and follow this through the forest to reach a road, opposite Druley Hill Farm.

Go left, down the road, to reach the farm lane to Brewham Lodge Farm, on the left. Ignore this, walking along the road for a further ²/₃ mile (1km) to reach a footpath on the left signed for Alfred's Tower. Take this path, following the hedge to the left to reach a fence. Go over the field beyond to reach a footbridge over the infant River

Brue and then bear left to reach Brewham Lodge Farm.

Go through the farm and bear right along a fence – which is to your left – towards the forest. Go through a gate into the forest and follow a forest track, bearing left where it forks. Where the track bends distinctly left, beyond the fork, go right on to a somewhat indistinct path and follow it to a stile. Go over the stile to reach the track followed on the outward journey. Go right and reverse the outward route back to **Alfred's Tower**.

POINTS OF INTEREST:

Hardway – The road from Redlynch to Alfred's Tower is marked as Hardway on the Ordnance Survey map. The Hardway is an old ridgeway, probably one of the earliest roads in Britain, that linked Dover with the centre of England. The name recurs in several places in England, and is almost certainly the basis of the name of Harrow, one of the country's most famous schools.

Kingswood Warren – The Warren is part of the old forest of Penselwood, mentioned in the Domesday book as a Royal Forest, that is one in which hunting was reserved for the King and his court. In the time of King Arthur this was *Coed Mawr*, the Great Wood, so large it could harbour a host of outlaws, a fact that made a journey through it a perilous venture. The Saxons did not pacify it, but they did change its name, to Selwood. The village in the wood then became Penselwood and later this name was applied to the wood itself. Order was finally brought to the wood by St Aldhelm, first Bishop of Shelbourne, who defied apparent good sense by travelling into the wood to convert the outlaws – and succeeded.

Alfred's Tower – After he had been defeated by the Danes, King Alfred retreated to Athelney, set among the Somerset Levels. There he and his men rested. Finally he led his men into the forest of Penselwood and set up his standard at a boundary marker called Egbert's Stone. Men rallied to him and he gathered an army of sufficient size and enthusiasm to defeat the Danes at Edgerley, near Glastonbury. Egbert's Stone is now gone, but in 1772 Henry Moore of Stourhead erected this brick tower close to the spot where Alfred's standard was raised, at the boundary of Somerset, Wiltshire and Dorset. The tower is 157 feet (48 metres) high and has a statue of the King in a niche above the door.

REFRESHMENTS:

None on route, but on Hardway between Redlynch and Alfred's Tower there is a fine inn, The Bull, at a cross-roads where the road to South Brewham heads north.

Walk 32   **BLAGDON LAKE**   4m (6½km)

Maps: OS Sheets Landranger 182; Pathfinder ST 45/55.
A walk on Mendip edge, with fine lake views.
Start: At 529583, the church at Ubley.

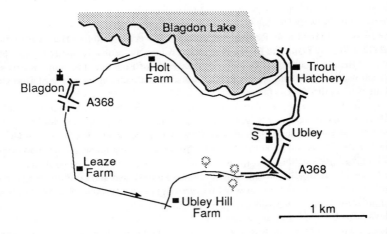

With your back to the church, facing Blagdon Lake, go right to the cross-roads near
the village cross. Go left and follow the lane gently downwards to reach a T-junction.
Turn left and follow the lane to the Ubley trout hatchery. Opposite the hatchery a
signed footpath heads towards the lake – ignoring, as you are instructed, the Water
Board track to the lake. The path actually runs parallel to the Water Board track and,
remarkably, does so all the way around the lake to Holt Farm, a distance of about
1½ miles (2½km). Beyond the farm the track continues along the water's edge, but
our route bears left and uphill to reach a lane. Turn right along the lane to reach a T-
junction. Turn left up Church Street and walk up to the main A368 road which bisects
Blagdon.

Cross the main road and go up Score Lane opposite. Continue up the lane until it
ends, then follow the path ahead up the Mendip edge. Go over a stile and follow the

hedge to the left to reach a gate. Go through and walk up the lane towards Leaze Farm. At a junction of tracks continue uphill, going to the right of the farm. After 150 yards go left into Leaze Lane and follow it as it contours along the hillside, with fine views to the north over Blagdon Lake and the country around Butcombe. Where the lane ends continue on a path across the hillside until Ubley Hill Farm is seen ahead. About 100 yards before the farm the path reaches a cross track. Turn left down this – it is called Ubley Drove – following it as it goes steeply down and bears right through Ubley Wood, a very pleasant section of woodland.

Beyond the wood the path reaches a lane. Continue down this to reach Lake View Cottage, to the right. Opposite the cottage there is a signed footpath. Take this, crossing a field to reach the main A368 again. Cross and go left for a few yards to reach a signed footpath to the right. Follow the path across a field to reach a stile. Go over and walk past bungalows to reach a road. Turn right and walk to **Ubley Church** and the start of the walk.

POINTS OF INTEREST:

Blagdon Lake – The lake is an artificial reservoir created in 1901. It is less well-known than its bigger neighbour, Chew Valley Lake, but is equally good for waterfowl watching and trout fishing.

Blagdon – This delightful village has maintained some of its Mendip character against the expansion of Bristol's professional classes. The church is beautifully set and has a magnificent 15th century tower.

Ubley Church – The church of St Bartholomew is 13th century and contains a superb Jacobean wooden pulpit, together with a chained copy of a very early gospel. The village cross is medieval, but restored.

REFRESHMENTS:

The Live and Let Live Inn, Blagdon.
The Queen Adelaide, Blagdon.
The New Inn, Blagdon.

Walk 33   THE RIVER PARRETT   4m (6½km)

Maps: OS Sheets Landranger 193; Pathfinder ST 41/51.

The eastern Levels, and a famous river, of Somerset.

Start: At 462192, All Saints' Church, Martock.

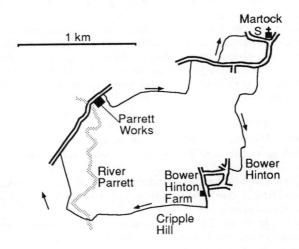

From the church head south down the B3165 passing through the finest section of Martock. The road turns right, and a road comes in, from the left, from Stoke Sub Hamden: go with the main road, but 50 yards beyond the corner go left on a footpath between houses to reach a Recreation Ground. Go across this to the far right-hand corner to reach a stile. Go over and follow the field edge, going over two more stiles to reach a path between trees. Go through a gate and follow the field edge to a stile. Go over on to a track. Turn right for 20 yards to reach a stile on the left. Cross and follow the right-hand hedge to a gate. Go through and walk ahead to reach a stile on the right. Go over on to a track to the main road in Bower Hinton.

Cross the road and go up Middle Street. At the top go left into Back Lane and along it to reach a track, going right, beyond Bower Hinton Farm. The track reaches a gate and stile. Go over and cross the flank of Cripple Hill, heading due west and going over several stiles, to reach a bridge. Cross this to reach a bridge over the **River Parrett**. Go over the bridge and turn right on to a path along the river's left bank. This section of the walk is on a Permissive Path, not a Right of Way, so it is important not to do anything that could prejudice the long term existence of the permission.

Go over a stile and head just right of the distant factory chimney to reach another stile in a hedge. Follow the left edge of the field ahead, then go to the left of a barn to reach a road. Turn right and walk to the Parrett Works, the factory seen earlier. Go past a caravan site and turn right through a gate to reach a path between a wall and a bungalow. Stay with the wall as you cross a field to reach a gate. Do not go through: instead turn left and follow the field edge to reach another gate. Go through and cross the field ahead to reach a stile on to a bridge. Go over and cross two fields to reach a track. Turn left along this to its junction with a road.

Turn right along the road, following it for 200 yards to reach a bridge on the left. Go over this and cross a field to a gap in its far hedge. Go through and turn right to another bridge. Cross the bridge and go right to reach a stile beneath a glorious cedar. Go over the stile and turn right down the lane to reach **All Saints' Church** and the start of the walk.

POINTS OF INTEREST:

Martock – The village, together with the hamlets of Hurst and Bower Hinton to the south, formed what was known as the Long village, a prosperous place in the 18th and 19th centuries when it was a centre for glove-making. The main street near the church has some fine buildings. The Treasurer's House – so called because an early Martock vicar had been treasurer of Wells Cathedral – is part 13th century, with 14th and 15th century modifications. The Market House is Georgian, and close to it is a fine 17th century Manor House. The 17th century Church House was once the court house.

River Parrett – The Parrett, which rises near the Somerset/Dorset border, flows through the Somerset Levels and Bridgwater, then forms a wide tidal estuary with the Bristol Channel, an estuary that was once an important port. The Parrett Works was an industrial complex in the 18th century.

All Saints' Church – The interior of the church is said by many to be the finest in Somerset for the excellence of its roof, and the exquisite contrast of the golden hamstone and the carved wood.

REFRESHMENTS:

The Bakers Arms, North Street, Martock.
The George, Church Street, Martock.
The Rose and Crown, Bower Hinton.

Walks 34 & 35   **HOLFORD**   4m (6$\frac{1}{2}$km) or 6m (9$\frac{1}{2}$km)
Maps: OS Sheets Landranger 181; Pathfinder ST 04/14.
Two walks that follow the wooded, eastern Quantock Combes.
Start: At 162382, the car park on the road to Crowcombe.

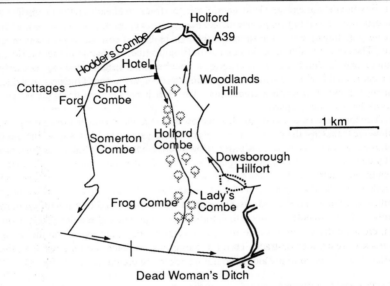

Only one road crosses the Quantock ridge, linking Nether Stowey to Crowcombe.
The car park is to the left about a mile east of Crowcombe Park Gate, close to where
another road joins from the right.

The start is close to **Dead Woman's Ditch**, the shallow, tree-lined ditch that runs
south of the car park. From the car park go north on the road that joins the cross-
Quantock road. Just after a sharp turn to the right a track leaves the road to the left:
take this and follow it to a junction of tracks. Turn left and follow the cross-track to
Dowsborough hill fort. There are several paths across the hill-fort. After using them
to explore the site make for the north-west corner (top right from your entry point)
where an obvious track heads across open hillside, with the next objective, Woodlands
Hill, visible to the north. The track is always obvious, but it is worth a few minutes of
study as the route bears left to go around the western side of the Hill, rather than the

eastern side. On the western side of the hill go over at a junction of paths, continuing to reach a road close to its junction with the main A39. Go left along the road towards Holford. Go around a sharp left bend and continue for 100 yards to reach an even sharper right bend. The longer route stays with the road here, but the shorter route goes left on a lane to Combe House, now a hotel, and Combe Cottages.

Beyond the cottages the lane deteriorates to a track and heads up the magnificent Holford Combe, staying very close to, and occasionally crossing, the combe's stream. At a very picturesque spot the stream divides (in reality, of course, two streams meet here). The stream to the right flows through Frog Combe, while that to the left flows through Lady's Combe. Our route goes into neither, choosing instead the southerly track between the two. This track emerges from trees on to the open Quantock hillside, bearing rightward to reach a cross track. Turn left here, the new track taking you directly back to the car park.

The longer route does not turn left, following the road to Holford Green car park. Follow the track past the houses to the west of the Green (i.e. to 'this side'). The track soon reaches woodland: stay on it, ignoring a turn right to Willoughby Cleeve. Go past a curious octagonal house – called The Round House, an equally curious name given the geometry – to reach the deep cleft of Hodder's Combe. The Combe's stream is forded close to the entrance to Short Combe, beyond which there is a junction of combes and paths. To the right is Shepperd's Combe, half-right is Slaughterhouse Combe, while half-left is Somerton Combe. Our route takes the latter. Follow the path, crossing the stream several times, to emerge on open ground. Continue along the track to reach a cross-track. Turn left along this, to reach the junction with the shorter route. Now continue along the track back to the car park.

POINTES OF INTEREST:

Dead Woman's Ditch – The story has it that John Walford, a Quantock charcoal-burner, was forced to marry a simpleton girl despite his love for another. Eventually he became so frustrated that he killed his wife in a drunken fury. He hid her body here, but it was discovered and he was tried and executed. His body was gibbetted at Walford's Gibbet, on the road from Nether Stowey.

Dowsborough – The name of this Iron Age hill fort could derive from Danesburgh, a local story having a Danish army encamped here before its routing by King Alfred. One Viking is said to have fallen in love with a local girl and to have been hidden by her after the battle. He was discovered and killed, but his ghost haunts the site.

REFRESHMENTS:
The Plough Inn, Holford.

Walk 36   **Compton Bishop**   4m (6¹/₂km)

Maps: OS sheets Landranger 182; Pathfinder ST 25/35 and ST 45/55.

A find ridge walk with expansive views.

Start: At 397554, Compton Bishop Church.

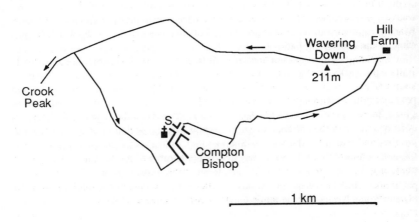

Go north along Church Lane, but where it goes right head straight on up a lane. The lane bears right to reach a gate. Go through and cross a yard to reach a field. Cross this to a gate, and cross the field beyond along its bottom edge to reach a stile. Go over and walk along the bottom edge of the next field. When your path reaches a cross track go left and up the track towards a wall. Take a stile over the wall and go up over rough ground, and past some fairly malevolent gorse bushes, bearing to the right towards a distinctive cluster of yew trees.

  Above the trees, the somewhat indistinct path contours around the hillside to reach Hill Farm. Close to the farm the route joins the West Mendip Way (*see* Note to Walk 66), the wide path that runs across the broad ridge of Wavering Down. Turn left along this path to reach the trig point on the Down. The summit here is only at 692 feet

(211 metres), while that of Crook Peak to the west is even lower at 626 feet (191 metres), yet the view from the top is remarkable. South-west are the Quantocks, the Brendons and Exmoor, with Dunkery Beacon visible on a clear day, while to the west is the Bristol Channel coast, with the Welsh coast beyond. Northward is the fine country south of Bristol. Only to the east, where the view is truncated by the remaining Mendip peaks, is the panorama limited.

Continue along the ridge path – where you can actually walk with your right foot in Avon and your left in Somerset – beside the wall, dropping down to the shallow col between Wavering Down and Crook Peak. The wall goes right, but our route continues up the hill ahead to reach the trig point on the summit of **Crook Peak**.

After enjoying the view from the Peak reverse the route back to the wall. There, go right on a downhill path which heads towards a white house. Follow the path through some excellent rough country of blackthorn and trees until a house is passed. Now turn sharp left into a lane in **Compton Bishop**. Follow this to a road and go left along the road back to the church.

POINTS OF INTEREST:

Crook Peak – From the M5 motorway Crook Peak is a distinctive hill, soaring above the traffic with its comma-like notched summit. Despite its dominant appearance the Peak is quite low, only 626 feet (191 metres) high. The name is said by some to derive from the summit which looks a little like a shepherd's crook, though it seems more likely that it comes from the rocky summit rib which looks like the crook saddle of a packhorse. Both the Peak and Wavering Down fall within the borders of an SSSI (Site of Special Scientific Interest) which covers 720 acres of grass, scrub and trees.

Compton Bishop – This is a delightful little hamlet nestling into a natural, protective, hollow of the high ridge. The church of St Andrew is early 13th century and houses a 14th century carved stone pulpit that is one of the best examples of its type in Somerset. An extra panel was added to the pulpit in the mid-19th century, by well meaning, but mistaken, 'restorers'. In the churchyard is the shaft of a 14th century cross.

REFRESHMENTS:

None on route, but the White Hart and the New Inn at Cross, where a road to Compton Bishop leaves the A38, at the bottom of Shute Shelve Hill, are only a couple of miles away.

NORTH HILL   4m (6¹/₂km)

Maps: OS Sheets Landranger 181; Pathfinder SS 84/94.
A fine coastal walk above Minehead.
Start: At 969473, the car park at Quay West, Minehead.

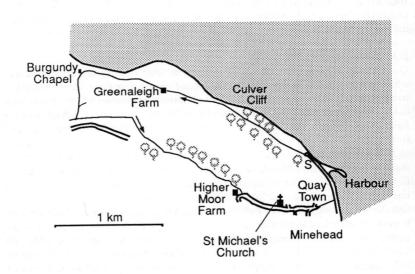

The car park is reached by driving along the sea front to Minehead's harbour and lifeboat station, and continuing to where the road ends below the woods of Culver Cliff.

From the car park, in **Quay Town**, walk to the road end and take the left-hand path, which is signed to Greenaleigh Farm. The path climbs up to cliff top level, then runs parallel with Culver Cliff all the way to the farm. Go through the farmyard and continue in the same direction to reach the ruins of **Burgundy Chapel**, tucked away on the right. At the chapel go left and follow the steep path up the somewhat unimmaginatively named Burgundy Chapel Combe. Towards the top of the Combe the **Somerset and North Deven Coastal Path** joins from the left. Follow this to the next path junction. Here the Coastal Path turns right, but our route goes left, heading back towards Minehead, on a path signed for the sea.

Follow the path to a small car park, turning right there on to a concrete track towards Moor Wood. Go into the wood and bear right at the edge of a concrete hardstanding. At the path junction ahead turn right, then go immediately left on a path signed for Higher Town. Follow this path downhill to reach a road to the right of Higher Moor Farm. Go left on the road, walking down it to pass **St Michael's Church**. Bear left at The Cross beyond the church and walk to the War Memorial. This stands on a hairpin bend: cross here and descend Church Path to the seafront. Turn left along the road to return to the start.

POINTS OF INTEREST:

Quay Town – This was once a village and port separate from Minehead, the town of which it is now a suburb. Indeed, in Domesday England only Quay Town existed, it being believed that the name of the larger town derives from *Mohun heved*, Mohun from the Norman family granted the local area by William the Conqueror, heved from the Saxon for headland. The harbour was a prosperous place in the 18th century, ships from America and the West Indies tying up here. Later, it was an important, and equally prosperous, fishing port and it is to that era that the elegant row of fishermen's cottages belongs. There is also a Fisherman's Chapel in an old cellar near the Quay. Fishing vessels still use the harbour, though much of the traffic now consists of pleasure boats.

Burgundy Chapel – The origins of the chapel, and its name, are shrouded in mysteries. It has been suggested that it was built in thanksgiving by a Somerset knight returning from active service in Burgundy. There is also a statement in the accounts of Dunster Castle for the year 1405 which suggests it was a summer house for the castle owners – though this would not explain the name. Whatever its origins, it has been ruinous for a century or more, though recently it has been stablilised to stop further decay.

Somerset and North Devon Coastal Path – The walk described here includes the first, or last, section of the South-West Peninsula Path, Britain's longest National Trail. The Path starts, or ends, at Quay Town.

St Michael's Church – The church is a fine one and houses a 15th century font, a 17th century carved pulpit and a beautiful long screen dated 1499. There is also a collection of rare books.

REFRESHMENTS:

Minehead has everything the walker could want, but the following two inns, in Quay Town, are very close to the start of the walk:-

The Old Ship Aground Inn, Quay Town.

The Red Lion Hotel, Quay Town.

Walk 38   **WESTHAY MOOR**   4m (6$\frac{1}{2}$km)

Maps: OS Sheets Landranger 182; Pathfinder ST 44/54.
A walk across the Somerset Levels.
Start: At 438428, the car park beside Westhay Bridge.

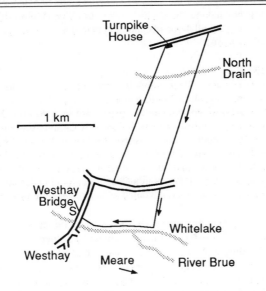

The car park lies to the left of the B3151, the main road from **Westhay** to Wedmore, just after Westhay Bridge has taken the walker over the River Brue.

Walk north along the road – there is no verge, so caution is required – to reach a road junction near Turnpike House. Go right on to the minor road to Godney. After about 300 yards a signed bridleway goes left, crossing **Westhay Moor** and bridging North Drain to reach a road. Go right, along the road, for 700 yards to reach another bridleway, this time to the right. This second bridleway runs parallel to the first, recrossing North Drain and Westhay Moor to reach the Godney road again. Cross the road and go up the track opposite, following the path beyond it to reach Whitelake, another river draining the Somerset Levels, one that once ran out of **Meare** pool. Go right and follow the river to its confluence with the River Brue. Continue along the river bank to reach Westhay Bridge. Cross the road to reach the car park.

POINTS OF INTEREST:

Westhay – Close to the village, in 1970, one of the world's oldest manufactured roads was discovered. The road, occasionally called the Sweet Track after its finder, Mr Roy Sweet of Westhay, was a duckboard path of wattle and poles. It is thought that the track is 6,000 years old, though it is not known whether it was laid in order to cross the Levels, or just to give access to them. Since the marshland would have been a natural defence, it is possible that villages were dotted about it.

Westhay Moor – It is planned to make the Moor a nature reserve to preserve the habitat of the swans, waterfowl, herons and kingfishers. However decisions will have to be taken about the peat-cutting on the Levels. To maintain the peat industry the water level of the Levels has to be dropped periodically, but this has a disastrous affect on water plants, animal life and bird populations.

Meare – The name derives from *mere*, this part of the Levels having once been completely submerged and farming a substantial pool. On the edge of this pool Iron Age folk built villages on stilts taking advantage – as their ancestors, the builders of the Sweet Track, had – of the area's natural defences and food supply. Later, in the 14th century, fishermen lived in the village with the sole purpose of catching, and salting down, fish for the monks of Glastonbury Abbey. The Meare Fish House is in the care of English Heritage, and can be visited at any reasonable time. Collect the key from Manor House Farm.

REFRESHMENTS:
The Bird in Hand, Westhay.

Walk 39   **CASTLE NEROCHE**   4m (6¹/₂km)

Maps: OS Sheets Landranger 193; Pathfinder ST 21/31.
An old castle on the edge of the Blackdowns.
Start: At 272157, the car park at Castle Neroche.

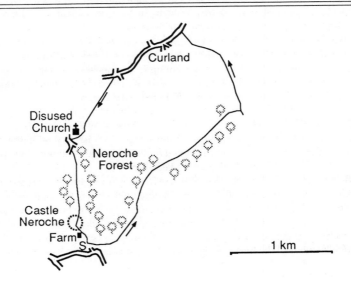

The car park is best reached from the B3170 south of Taunton. About 8 miles (13 kms) south of Corfe, take the turn to the left for Broadway and Horton. After 2¹/₂ miles (4 kms), go left for Curland and Staple Fitzpaine, turning right shortly after, and then going left for the Nature Trail. The car park is now to the left.

From the car park go east up the slope to reach a fence and the first red waymarker. Follow the waymarkers steeply down through the forest to reach a gate at a track junction. Go through and follow the bridlepath ahead. Go ahead again at the next gate on a path along the edge of the forestry plantation (which is on your right). The path ends at a gate on to a track. Go through and left, along the track, ignoring all turns to left and right to reach a road.

Go left along the road to the village of Curland. Pass the Post Office, on the right, and bear left at the triangle just after. Continue along the road to reach the

Equestrian Centre, on the right. Opposite this turn left through a gate on to a path along the right-hand hedge of a field. Follow this hedge across two more fields. A stile is reached in the far corner of the third field: go over and follow the path along the left-hand hedge of two further fields, to reach a gate in a corner. Go through the gate, and follow the hedge to another. Go through and turn left down a track past a now disused church. Beyond the church the track reaches a road close to a T-junction. Turn left to the junction, and go right at it.

After only about 50 yards go left through a gate to reach a steep, and somewhat stony, path up through a section of the **Neroche Forest**, ignoring all turns to the left and right. Go through a gate and turn right up steps, following a yellow waymarker. This leads to a viewpoint over **Castle Neroche**, which can be reached by going down steps and across a bridge. From it, go left to reach the start of the walk.

POINTS OF INTEREST:

Neroche Forest – In medieval times the forest was much larger than it is at present, and was a Royal Forest, that is one reserved for the King and his court. Local peasants found poaching in the forest would have been hanged.

Castle Neroche – This impressive hillfort is Iron Age in origin, but was also used by the Normans who improved its defences. Invariably the Normans are associated with stone castles, but after their conquest of England they initially built motte and bailey castles – earthworks defended by stout stockades. It is likely that Castle Neroche, with its existing defensive walls, was pressed into early service before the Normans had finally subdued the locals. From the castle five counties are said to be visible.

REFRESHMENTS:

None on route, but the nearby village of Staple Fitzpaine – a very pretty little village whose church has a beautiful 15th century tower – has an inn.
The Greyhound Inn, Staple Fitzpaine.

Walk 40   **PRIDDY POOLS**   4m (6¹/₂km)

Maps: OS Sheets Landranger 182; Pathfinder ST 45/55.
A short, but historically interesting, outing.
Start: At 548515, the roadside park beside the larger pool.

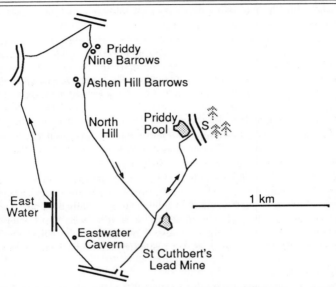

Walk the few yards to the edge of the largest of the **Priddy Pools**, then go left along
its edge. Turn right along the old dam at its southern end, taking great care with the
airy step over the old sluice gate opening. At the dam's end go left on a well-walked
path that heads across hummocky ground to reach a broader track. Go right on this,
following it past the second of the Priddy Pools. Continue along the track, with the
ruins of old mines – **St Cuthbert's** – to the left, to reach a road near some houses.

Go right, past the houses, for about 200 yards to reach a gate on the right. Go
through and cross the field beyond diagonally leftward towards a farm. The path
passes the entrance to **Eastwater Cavern** to reach a lane. Go right to Eastwater Farm,
beyond which a clear bridlepath – Eastwater Drove – continues in the same direction
to reach a road. Go right, but after 150 yards leave the road through a gate to the right.
The next objectives are the **Priddy Nine Barrows** on top of the ridge ahead. The right-

76

of-way actually goes diagonally left to reach a gate in the far left corner of the field, then turns through 135° to walk due south to the barrows. Walkers have been known to forego this seemingly pointless route in favour of a direct approach – but it is not a right-of-way.

From the barrows head due south along the ridge to a second group of barrows (the Ashen Hill Barrows). Go through the gate in the field corner ahead and follow the path beside the wall downhill to reach the second of the pools passed on the outward journey. Go left and retrace the route back to the start.

POINTS OF INTEREST:

Priddy Pools – The largest of the pools, where the walk starts, is more accurately called Waldegrave Pool, but most people, even most Mendip dwellers, now use the more obvious name. The pools are home to legions of toads and newts, in season, and are an important site for breeding dragonflies. The ground around the pools, especially the old walls, is popular with adders so it is advisable to be careful if you have young children with you. The marshy ground is equally popular with grass snakes. Close to the start point there is an excellent stand of Scots Pine, looking rather more picturesque than the conifer plantation across the road.

St Cuthbert's Lead Mine – St Cuthbert's was one of the most important of Mendip lead mines, and was responsible for the hummocks passed by the route. This type of hummocky scenery is known locally as gruffy ground. The ruins include those of several horizontal flues. Lead ore was roasted to smelt out the metal, but the mine owners also retrieved metallic lead that was carried in the furnace smoke. This was deposited on the walls of the horizontal flues and scraped off by men after the smoke had cleared. Lead mining and smelting was a dirty, dangerous job, lead poisoning taking its toll of the workers, but this job must have been the most unpleasant,.

Eastwater Cavern – This tortuous and unstable cave is one of the deepest on Mendip, going down over 400 feet.

Priddy Nine Barrows – These barrows, and the nearby Ashen Hill group, are Bronze Age round barrows constructed as burial mounds for the cremated remains of the dead.

REFRESHMENTS:

None on the route, but the start lies between the Castle of Comfort and the Hunter's Lodge Inns, each of them about $1^1/_4$m (2 km) away. There are also inns in Priddy village.

Walk 41   **BLAISE CASTLE**   4$\frac{1}{2}$m (7km)

Maps: OS Sheets Landranger 172; Pathfinder ST 47/57.

A fine country walk within the Bristol city boundary.

Start: At 558788, Blaise Castle car park.

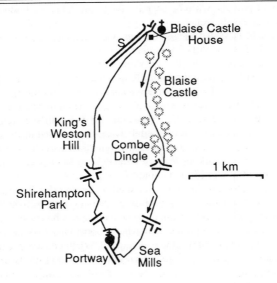

From the car park walk through the **Blaise Castle Estate** to reach the Folk Museum. Go out of the estate along the drive and turn right immediately into Church Lane, going right again soon after to reach the church of St Mary. Go to the right of the church to reach steps which lead down through a tunnel to a bridge over the River Trym. Cross the bridge and turn right to reach Stratford Mill. The route now follows the metalled drive which runs parallel with the river through the wooded and rock outcrop studded Blaise Castle estate. Some of the rock outcrops have fanciful names – Lover's Leap, Goram's Chair etc. but are no less impressive for that. Goram is a legendary giant who inhabited the wood, and also gives his name to the Giant's Soap Dish, another distinctive feature.

Continue along the metalled drive, ignoring all side turns and bridges until a distinctive oval pond is reached. Take the next bridge over the river and continue with the water on your left hand. When a road is reached go right on it, but left almost immediately on a path which goes under another road in Combe Dingle. Cross the river at the next bridge and go right on a path that follows it to reach a road close to Mill House Inn. Go right across the front of the inn, then cross the road to reach a path which leads to the river again. The narrow path soon reaches a wide meadow and a fine single row of poplars, with the busy Portway (the A4) on a low viaduct ahead. Follow the river to the viaduct.

The path can be followed under the Portway to reach an old harbour on the River Avon. This was the Roman port of *Abonae*: more recently it represented the last point on the river that could be reached before ships had to wait for a high tide. The local area is called Sea Mills, after old tidal mills which used to operate on the river. Our route does not visit the old harbour but crosses the Trym by footbridge and follows a steep path, to the left, to reach the Portway. Turn right, then right again into Riverleaze, bearing left with the road to reach The Pentagon and St Edyth's church. Go left into Avonleaze, then right on a signed footpath between houses that leads to Three Acre Covert. Follow the edge of a small wood to the right, then cross Sylvan Way to reach a stile into Shirehampton Park, now a golf course. Keep to the right edge of the park to reach a gate on to a road (Shirehampton Road). Across the road is Park Lodge: cross to it and go up its right side to reach a road (Kings Weston Road). Cross this to reach a metalled path and follow this to a footbridge back over the road. Do not cross: instead, turn away from the bridge on the wide path across Kings Weston Hill.

Go past the radio masts, continuing to where the path narrows and reaches a gate into woodland on the left. Go down the path beyond. When you emerge from the trees maintain direction across the open grass to reach the wood again. Bear right on the widest path to reach open ground and **Blaise Castle**. Beyond the tower bear left when the woods are re-entered, going downhill steeply – steps at one point – to reach open grass again. Cross this to reach the car park.

POINTS OF INTEREST:
Blaise Castle Estate – Blaise Castle House was built by John Scandrett, an 18th century Quaker banker. The estate grounds were landscaped by Repton, whose work was greatly aided by the natural beauty of the site.
Blaise Castle – The 'castle' is an 18th century folly tower built to look like a medieval ruin. In this it was helped by the ravages of time, though it has lately been stabilized as it was becoming dangerous.

REFRESHMENTS:
The Mill House Inn, Sea Mills.

Walk 42   **DULVERTON**   4½m (7km)

Maps: OS Sheets Landranger 181; Pathfinder SS 82/92.
A fine walk from a delightful town.
Start: At 913279, the car park beside Exmoor House, Dulverton.

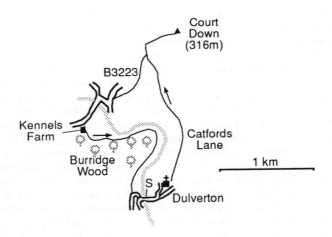

From **Exmoor House** go down to the main road and turn left into Bridge Street. Bear left into Fore Street and walk along this to **All Saints' Church**. Go into the churchyard, leaving it at its eastern end through a pair of iron gates. Go left up a narrow passage and then left again to pass the school and join a rough track. The track climbs steeply, but levels out as an attractive enclosed path called Catfords Lane. Follow the lane to its end at a gate, where another lane goes off to the left. Go through the gate and bear right on a path beside a hedge to reach another gate. Go through and continue along the path to the trig point summit of **Court Down**.

Retrace your steps to the gate at the end of Catfords Lane. Go through and turn right down the lane towards Marsh Bridge. Ignore turnings to right and left to reach a road. Go left, and immediately right on a minor road for Draydon and Hawkridge, in the process going over **two bridges**. At the junction about 150 yards further on turn

80

left – on the Hawkridge road – over the River Barle. Walk along the road for 250 yards to reach the lane, to the left, for Kennels Farm, so named because it was once the kennels for the Northmoor Hunt. Go past the left side of the farm to reach a signed path that goes through Burridge Wood to reach the River Barle. The path stays close to the river and reaches a lane. Follow the lane to a road and turn left to return towards **Dulverton**. At a T-junction go left into Bridge Street. Go over the River Barle and turn left to regain Exmoor House.

POINTS OF INTEREST:

Exmoor House – This striking building was built as the Dulverton Workhouse in 1855, for the princely sum of £2,811. It housed 52 poor folk from all over the surrounding Exmoor area. Amazingly the building continued to house folk until 1930, and even after that it was used as a centre for local girls training to be domestics. This continued until 1939. After the War, the building served as a maternity hospital until, in 1974, it became the headquarters of the Exmoor National Park Authority.

All Saints' Church – The church tower is 12th century, though all of the rest of the church was built in the 1850s. Beside the tower is the stump of the Belfry Tree, a sycamore at least 200 years old that was struck by lightning many years ago, 'repaired' by tree surgeons, but finally blown over in 1975. It is a famous local landmark.

Court Down – The high point of the down, at 1,036 feet (316 metres) is a tremendous vantage point with Dartmoor and the Blackdown Hills being visible. Inevitably, though, the eye is drawn to the beautiful wooded valleys of the Barle and the Exe.

Two Bridges – Marsh Bridge, over the Barle, is an iron girder bridge, most unusual for this area where bridges are normally stone. The Barle tributary is crossed by a more usual pack-horse bridge.

Dulverton – The town is delightful, and as the spot where John Ridd first saw Lorna Doone is assured of its place in Exmoor's history. The bridge over the Barle, a beautiful five-arched structure, is one of the oldest on Exmoor. Exmoor House and the town church are dealt with above, but other buildings are worth a look. The Town Hall in Fore Street – passed on the walk – dates from 1866 and has an external stairway designed by Sir Edward Luytems in 1927. At the eastern end of the town, beyond the Rock House Inn, Woodliving is a beautiful thatched cottage with tall chimneys, believed to have been built in the 13th century.

REFRESHMENTS:

There are many opportunities in Dulverton, but of special note are:-
The Rock House Inn, Jury Road, Dulverton.
The Copper Kettle, Fore Street, Dulverton.

Walk 43   **PINKWORTHY POND**   5m (8km)

Maps: OS Sheets Landranger 180; Pathfinder SS 64/74.
A difficult walk, but worthwhile.
Start: At 728402, on the B3358 near Driver Farm.

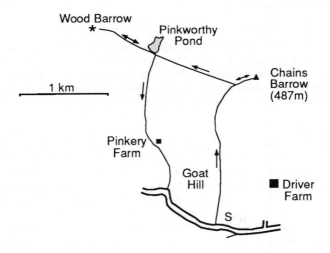

Cars can be parked in small verge pull-ins to the west of the lane to Driver Farm, on the B3358 that links Simonsbath to Challacombe.

Note: This walk is remote and crosses difficult ground. If the walker gets off route he could become lost if visibility is poor. If you are inexperienced in the use of map and compass, and in moorland walking, do not attempt the walk in poor weather.

Walk back towards the farm lane, and go through the gate on the left. Now go across two fields following the hedge on the right to reach a gate with a yellow waymarker. In the large field ahead there are several marker posts giving the direction to a gate in a wall. Beyond this is the open moor. Follow the track half-right towards the trig point sat on **Chains Barrow**, which is now clearly visible. Walk to the barrow.

The next objective is Pinkworthy Pond, north-west across the moor. This area of Exmoor is called The Chains and has a deserved reputation for being rough and difficult, a mix of peat bog and tussock grass. Therefore, go back to the wall and turn right along it, staying with it all the way to **Pinkworthy Pond**.

From the Pond's western edge follow the path – which is rather more of a scar on the landscape due to the erosion of years of walkers – that heads westward to reach Woodbarrow Gate, which sits on the border between Somerset and Devon. Go through to reach **Wood Barrow**. Return to Pinkworthy Pond along the same route and turn south (right) on the path that runs on the eastern (left) bank of the River Bank. The path uses logs and bridges to cross the boggy land beside the river, but persevere, beyond a stile there is firmer ground all the way to Pinkery Farm – the pond is pronounced Pinkery, the farm having given up the struggle and spelling its name as it sounds – now an outdoor centre for Somerset County Council. From the farm take the lane down to the road and turn left along the verge to return to the start.

POINTS OF INTEREST:

Chains Barrow – Chains is a Bronze Age burial mound of which there are many in this area of Exmoor. Its existence implies that the climate was warmer in the Bronze Age, with folk living on the moor rather than at its edge. The builders of the mound clearly wanted it to be seen, and it is so conspicuous on its high point that it has been used to support an ordnance survey trig point. From the barrow Dunkery Beacon and Dartmoor can be seen.

Pinkworthy Pond – The pond was created in 1837 when John Knight, who owned most of Exmoor, imported 200 Irish labourers to build a dam. Exactly why Knight wanted the pond is not clear. Theories include the provision of a guaranteed source of irrigation water for local farms, but this seems unlikely in an area that attracts 80 inches of rain annually. Others say it was to power waterwheels in a projected iron ore mine, but that seems no more likely. Perhaps he just wanted a pond. The pond is said to be haunted by the ghost of a local farmer who drowned himself in it in 1889.

Wood Barrow – The barrow is another Bronze Age burial mound, said to be protected by natural spirits after a group of locals, digging for the treasure that legend had it lay within the mound, were frightened off by thunder and lightning.

REFRESHMENTS:

None on route, but there are inns in Simonsbath and Challacombe, each just a couple of miles away.

Walk 44 BRUNEL'S BRIDGE AND LEIGH WOODS 5m (8km)
Maps: OS Sheets Landranger 172; Pathfinder ST 47/57.

A walk that links history and the exquisite woodland of the Avon Gorge.

Start: At 565735, on the Clifton Down Road side, close to the Percival Road junction.

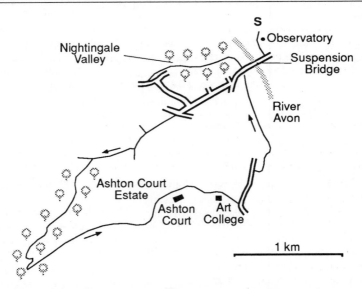

From Clifton Down Road take the metalled path, or climb the grassy slopes, to reach the **Observatory** at the summit of Clifton Down. From it the path continues along the Gorge edge – there are railings – past the top of an inclined slab of rock worn smooth by the backsides of generations of sliding children. Eventually an exit right can be made to the road and Brunel's **Suspension Bridge**.

Cross the bridge – a toll is payable, and the bridge is not for those who are fearful of heights – to reach Bridge Road. Walk to the end of Bridge Road, where it joins the main A369 road. Across the road is the lodge and gateway of Ashton Court. Cross the main road with care and go through the lodge and along the drive. To the right here is a pitch and putt course, while to the left Bristol can be seen between the trees.

84

Ignore the first drive to the right, which leads to the golf course car park, but take the second. The drive soon reaches woods to the left. When the wood edge falls away to the left go with it. Stay with the wood, entering it through a gap in the fence – look for the fallen tree – to reach a post marked NT4. This is on the route of the deer park Nature Trail. Now follow the trail, going right, close to the old fencing of the deer park. At NT10 bear left and follow the zig-zag path downhill. At the bottom go left on the narrow track near the wall – **not** on the broad track – passing a pool. Pass Clarken Combe Lodge and continue on the drive through the park. There, to the left beyond the fence, the park's fallow deer can usually be seen.

Go right at a T-junction of paths. Follow the drive that goes left past Ashton Court. Soon, this goes downhill past one of Bristol's Art Colleges – to the right – and reaches the main road. Cross and go left along the edge of the cricket ground. At its end go right along an enclosed path. Cross the railway to reach the Avon's bank. Go left towards the Suspension Bridge. Go under the bridge and take the first turning left, going under a railway bridge to reach Nightingale Valley. The valley is climbed to the top of the gorge, the path going through the superb Leigh Woods. At the top the valley path reaches North Road. Go left to reach Bridge Road. Now go left to reach the Suspension Bridge, following the outward journey back to the start.

POINTS OF INTEREST:

Observatory – The observatory is not a folly, but the only remaining part of a snuff mill which was burnt down in the late 18th century. The name derives from the late 1820's when a *camera obscura* was installed in it by one William West. West's device cast a 360° panorama of the local area on to a viewing table. Visits to the site were much prized for the illicit view of courting couples on the Downs. Sadly the *camera obscura* is not functioning at present.

The observatory also gave, and still gives, access to an underground passage which leads to the Giant's Cave, an opening high in the Avon Gorge's rocky wall. The view of the Suspension Bridge, the river and the rock climbers is superb.

Suspension Bridge – The bridge was built with money left by William Vick, a Bristol wine merchant, in 1752, though it was not until the 1830s that work, to a design by Isambard Kingdom Brunel, started. Money ran out in 1840, and work did not start again until 1859, after Brunel's death. The bridge was finally opened on 8 December 1864. It is 234 yards long, and 246 feet above the river level.

REFRESHMENTS:

Ashton Court has a restaurant and café and there are numerous ice cream sellers on Clifton Down.

Walk 45   **THE RIVER EXE**   5m (8km)

Maps: OS Sheets Landranger 181; Pathfinder SS 83/93.

A walk along Exmoor's most famous river.

Start: At 853366, beside the B3223 road south of Herne's Barrow.

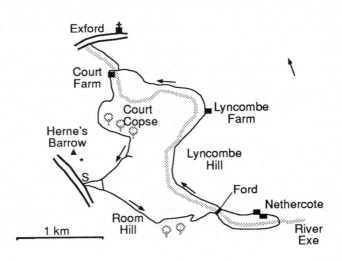

The B3223 Exford to Dulverton road climbs across fine moorland from Chibbet Post to Comer's Cross. To the left here is a trig point-topped summit close to Herne's Barrow, a Bronze Age burial mound. About 400 yards beyond the summit there is a signed path to the left. Park on the verge pull-ins here.

    Take the path that heads south-east along a beech hedge, going towards Room Hill – not that signed for Exford, that is the return route. Go over at a path junction and follow the path ahead as it descends into a small combe head, then rises across the flank of Room Hill. As a wood is approached, and close to a gate in the hedge, go left down a stony path that steepens as it falls towards the River Exe. Where the path reaches the Exe the river can be forded in most circumstances, but this does mean risking wet feet. When the river is high, or the spirit of adventure low, a 1 mile (1½km) detour is required going east (right as approached) to a bridge beyond the Nethercote farms, and returning along the opposite bank. Once over the river go west along a bankside path which goes around Lyncombe Hill to reach Lyncombe Farm.

Follow yellow waymarkers through the farm, bearing left beyond it on to a path that crosses marshy ground, using two stiles, to reach a gate on the right. Go through the gate and follow a path to another gate. Go through and diagonally across a field to reach a junction of paths. Go left through a gate and cross a field with a small natural mound on the left. Ignore a turn to the right and continue to reach the river again, opposite Court Farm. A detour to the right here, along the river bank, reaches **Exford** after about 500 yards.

Cross the bridge and go left through Court Farm. Go left off the track beyond, following a hedge to the top of a field. Bear left on a track at the top and follow it as it bends to the left to reach Court Copse. Follow the track along the wood edge, then continue to reach a gate. Go through and turn right on a path that climbs Road Hill along a beech hedge. At a path junction the path on the left goes across to reach the outward route, so bear right to return to the start.

POINTS OF INTEREST:

Exford – This beautiful little village typifies Exmoor, with its delightful houses, old bridge over the river that names the moor, and a surrounding circle of high moorland. The church, a somewhat sombre building, has been heavily (and not too well) restored. Inside, the best feature is a 15th century screen that was removed from St Audrey's Church in West Quantoxhead, when that was demolished, and re-erected here. In August the Exford Horse Show is worth visiting to see the best Exmoor ponies.

REFRESHMENTS:

The Crown Hill, Exford.
Exmoor House, the National Park Centre, also has a tea room in summer.

Walk 46   **CULBONE**   5m (8km)

Maps: OS Sheets Landranger 181; Pathfinder SS 84/94.
A walk on the Coastal Path.
Start: At 858483, the car park at Ashley Combe toll gate.

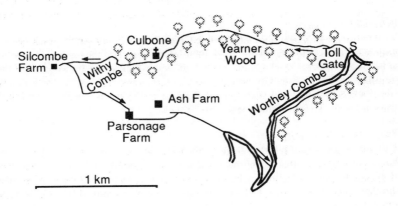

West of Porlock Weir a toll road goes through the delightful, wooded Worthy Combe.
The Somerset and North Devon section of the South-West Coastal Path comes this
way too, but walkers are exempt from the toll!

From the toll gate the Coastal Path heads west into **Yearner Wood**, a wood so
dense that even in summer it can offer dark, shadowy walking. There are occasional
views, however, taking in the Welsh coast across the Bristol Channel. The path bears
left into Culbone Combe and climbs to reach the isolated church of **Culbone**.

The path goes along the church wall, passing a gate into the churchyard, then
turns westward to cross the stream. Follow the Coastal Path waymarkers into Withy
Combe. At the end of the woodland a gate gives access to a lane which is followed to
a Y-junction close to Silcombe.

Turn sharply back left and follow the lane into, and out of, Withy Combe, continuing along it to reach Parsonage Farm. Go past the farm, turning left with the lane to reach a Y-junction where the lane to Ash Farm goes off left. Go right and follow the lane to reach a road junction. Go over and follow the road for 250 yards, then bear left on a lane. Follow the lane to a T-junction. Go left on a road, crossing Yearner Mill Bridge to reach a signed bridleway on the right. Take this, following it down through the beautiful Worthy Combe to reach a road. Go left back to the Toll Gate and car park.

POINTS OF INTEREST:

Yearner Wood – In the early medieval period the wood, then known as Kitner, was used as a prison, a mini-Australia where families who had offended against the church, as heretics, or against the state, as dissidents, were sent to live out a miserable existence on pain of death should they attempt to leave. The woods were used in this way for two periods, each of about 40 years, and in each case all of those incarcerated within its confines died. Later, the woods were used as a leper colony. Such thoughts, added to the dark, brooding atmosphere of the wood, can make it seem a sombre place. Perhaps it is better to dwell on its later use as a home to charcoal burners.

Culbone – The church here is claimed to be the smallest in England (and as such holds the strange record of being the only church to appear in both the Domesday Book and the Guinness Book of Records). It is dedicated to St Bruno, a Celtic saint, the name being derived from that of the saint. Today it seems a pleasant enough place, but years ago it was a formidable place to reach, the journey being across wild and dangerous country. An old Exmoor rhyme notes that:–

> Culbone, Oare and Stoke Pero
> The parishes there where no person 'll go.

REFRESHMENTS:

None on route, but there are inns and cafés in nearby Porlock Weir and Porlock.

Walk 47   **STRATTON-ON-THE-FOSSE**   5m (8km)

Maps: OS Sheets Landranger 183; Pathfinder ST 64/74 and
ST 65/75.

A pleasant walk at the edge of Somerset coal field.

Start: At 659508, the church in Stratton.

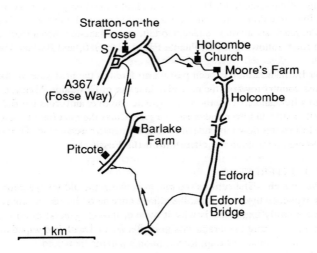

From the church go eastwards, out of the village, and take the first turn to the right, on
to the road to Holcombe. Go over a little bridge, across a stream which flows through
the elegantly named Snail's Bottom, and follow the road for another 200 yards to
reach a lane to the left. Take this and cross a field to reach a stile and gate. Go over
and bear right to reach a stile into Holcombe Wood. Keep to the path through the
wood – the notices imply dire retribution to anyone who dares to stray off line –
emerging to reach little **Holcombe Church** set in a cluster of cypress trees.

From the church take the metalled lane to Moore's Farm. Go through the farmyard
and down the farm lane to reach a road on a bend. You are turning left, though it feels
like you are walking ahead. At a T-junction go right and follow the road into Holcombe
village. Walk through the village, taking the main road – signed for Edford and Stoke

St Michael. Follow the road through the hamlet of **Edford** and on towards Edford Bridge. The route does not reach the bridge – though it is only a short detour to it, and the Duke of Cumberland Inn beside it – going right just before it, over a stile opposite a white house. Follow the path which runs parallel to the stream at first, but then bears slightly right to follow the edge of a wood.

Follow the wood edge through a field to reach a road near a bridge over the stream. Do not go out on to the road: instead, turn right to follow another wood along the far edge of the same field. The path now climbs steadily: go over seven stiles and maintain the same direction until a garden wall is reached. Go right, following this new wall to reach a gate on to a lane. Go left, up the lane to reach a road. Turn right along the road, following it past Pitcote Farm, to the left, and Barlake Farm, to the right.

After Barlake Farm has been passed, go through the next gate on the left, and head across country towards the now visible tower of Downside Abbey. Go through a gate into a field and cross to the stile opposite. Go over and cross the field ahead to reach another stile. Go over and cross to a gate. Cross the next field to reach a rutted track and follow this down the side of farm buildings to reach a road. Turn right along the road to regain the church in **Stratton-on-the-Fosse.**

POINTS OF INTEREST:

Holcombe church – The curious separation between the old village church and the village is explained by the fact that the village once stood beside the church, but has moved. Less easily explained is why it moved, though general opinion favours a repositioning in a more favourable position after Black Death had wiped out the first villagers. In the churchyard Capt Robert Scott's parents lie buried.

Edford – The difficulty of road transport of coal from the local mines led to a decision, last century, to dig a canal from the coal field to Frome. Work started, but was never finished. Close to the walk at Edford there is a prepared section of the canal, and other sections can be found in the wood to the left of the route from Edford.

Stratton-on-the-Fosse – The village stands beside the Roman Fosse Way and has a church with a very unusual dedication – to St Vigor. Downside Abbey was built in the early 19th century, the church beside it having been completed only in 1935. The windows are excellent examples of early 20th century artwork, a fairly rare sight.

REFRESHMENTS:
The King's Arms, South Street, Stratton-on-the-Fosse.
The White Post Inn, Stratton-on-the-Fosse.
The Duke of Cumberland, Edford Bridge.

Walk 48   **THE OUTSKIRTS OF TAUNTON**   5m (8km)
Maps: OS Sheets Landranger 193; Pathfinder ST 02/12 and
ST 22/32.
An interesting walk only a mile from the centre of Taunton.
Start: At 212265, the church in Staplegrove.

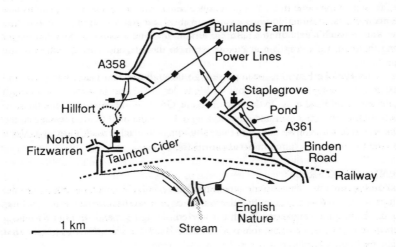

Staplegrove is a village suburb of Taunton, reached by turning right off the A358
Watchet road about 1 mile (1¹/₂ kms) north-west of Taunton's centre.

From the church walk back towards the main A358 and take a footpath over a
stile to the left, signed for Burlands. Go along the field edge to reach another stile. Go
over and follow the path over two more stiles before descending across several fields
to reach a road close to Burlands Farm. Turn left and follow the road to its T-junction
with the A358. Cross the road, with great care, particularly if there are children in
your party, and go right for a few yards, to reach a gate and a signed path for Norton
Fitzwarren. The path climbs up beneath the power lines to the **Norton Hillfort**. Bear
left around the fort to reach the sign for it. Go left there, taking the right-hand of two
paths down to a road. Cross the road to reach the churchyard and go through this and

down a lane to a road opposite the inn. Turn right into **Norton Fitzwarren**, taking the first left (Station Road) to pass the **Taunton Cider** works. At the end of the road go over the railway by footbridge and turn left on a path beside the railway lines. When a stream is reached the path bears right with it, away from the railway. Go over several stiles to reach a road. Go left to a T-junction. Cross and go up the lane opposite. Turn left at a T-junction, and right at another to reach the Headquarters of English Nature.

Beyond the English Nature building do not take the obvious track ahead: instead, go left along a narrower path to reach another on a raised bank. Turn right and follow the railway line, passing some allotments to reach the main road. Turn left and go over the railway. Turn left along Binden Road. Walk past Dowell Close to reach a footpath, on the right, and follow it to reach the main road again. Cross, with care, and take the path to the right of the village hall, passing a duck pond to the right. When Manor Road is reached turn left to reach the church and the start of the walk.

POINTS OF INTEREST:

Norton Hillfort – The hillfort is Iron Age, the last occupation being around 400 AD, although excavations have revealed that the site was occupied from the Stone Age.

Norton Fitzwarren – The church is worth a visit to see the carved screen whose frieze tells the story of the dragon that, legend has it, once lived in the hillfort above the village. The dragon made itself unpopular by occasionally descending to the village to add children to its menu. Finally, the local squire, Fulke Fitzwarren, went up to the hillfort and killed the dragon, in the best tradition of knighthood. The screen is excellent, and it can only be wondered why an early Victorian rector felt it so out of keeping with the church that he had it removed. Thankfully, a later vicar found it in a local junk shop and had it restored.

Taunton Cider – The works has a Visitor's Centre where the process, and history, of cider making is explained, and a shop where the end product can be bought.

REFRESHMENTS:

The Staplegrove Inn, Staplegrove.
The Ring of Bells, Norton Fitzwarren.
The Cross Keys, Norton Fitzwarren.

Walk 49   **ASHTON COURT**   5m (8km)

Maps: OS Sheets Landranger 172; Pathfinder ST47/57.
A country walk within sight of the Bristol City Centre.
Start: At 553710, the Angel Inn, Long Ashton.

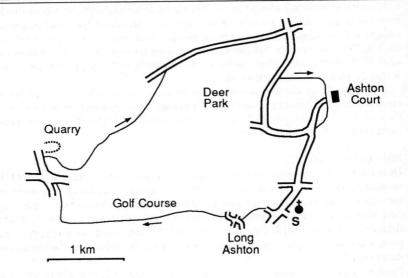

From the inn head towards Long Ashton village – that is away from the ornate entrance to Ashton Court. After about 250 yards go right into Hobwell Lane, which is signed for Long Ashton Golf Course. At its end go through a gate and bear left on a path. At the field corner bear left again, following the hedge to a gate. Go through on to an enclosed path and follow it to Folleigh Drive. Go along this, then right into Folleigh Lane which heads uphill. At the end take the footpath – signed for the Golf Course – which continues uphill. Go over a stile and bear right, still climbing, to reach a path fork. Go right on the path through the bracken to the top of the hill.

    Cross the fairway ahead – beware of golf balls – and pass a pond to the left. Ahead now are a group of trees: go left here along the Golf Course edge ignoring all paths on the right, to reach the extremity of the Course. There, with an open field to the right, take the path which heads downhill to the right. At the next path junction turn left through the old quarry to reach Providence Lane. Go right to a cross-roads. Go over, into Longwood Lane. Soon you reach a quarry to the left: opposite its entrance turn right into a wood. Go right almost immediately on to the broad Pill Grove.

Turn left at the Washout sign, following a parallel path when this path fades. Ignore all crossing paths until the one you are on, which narrows, reaches a wood and a high bank to the left. There go left, following the fence to a gap in it. Go half-right here, heading across the path to the wood on its far side. Follow the broad path at its edge to a T-junction. Go right on a broad avenue, with beautiful views of Bristol to the left. When the avenue reaches a metalled drive go right. The drive reaches the edge of the **deer park** – where fallow deer can usually be seen. At the edge go left across the park to reach **Ashton Court**.

Pass the Court and go down steps into the formal gardens. Go through these to reach the metalled drive again and follow it to the ornate gateway seen at the start of the walk. Go through and cross the main road to reach Long Ashton Road. The starting point is just along the road, to the left.

POINTS OF INTEREST:

Deer Park – The grounds of Smyth's Ashton Court estate, which extends to over 800 acres, were landscaped by Repton in the late 18th century. To him we owe many of the oaks and sweet chestnut trees. Originally the park was also a deer park, though the deer were later hunted to extinction. When the entire estate was taken over by the Bristol City Council in 1959 the deer were reintroduced, though only in part of the park, and enclosed by a high deer fence. Walkers will be unlucky not to see fallow deer beyond the fence.

Ashton Court – The Court was built in the 1630s by Thomas Smyth, a local MP. The frontage is almost 100 yards long and is certainly imposing, if not exactly beautiful. Some experts detect the hand of Inigo Jones in the work – especially in the south-west wing. However, others pour scorn on this idea, suggesting that the curious mix of styles – elements of Jacobean and Gothic, and even Tudor can be seen – is not at all in the master's mould. As an aside, Thomas Smyth – whose family originated in the Forest of Dean and were successful merchants – was one of the last country gentlemen in the area to have employed a full-time jester.

REFRESHMENTS:
The Angel Inn, Long Ashton.
Ashton Court has a restaurant and café.

Walk 50   **WEST BAGBOROUGH AND WILL'S NECK**   5m (8km)
Maps: OS Sheets Landranger 181; Pathfinder ST 03/13.
A walk to the highest Quantock summit.
Start: At 170334, the centre of West Bagborough.

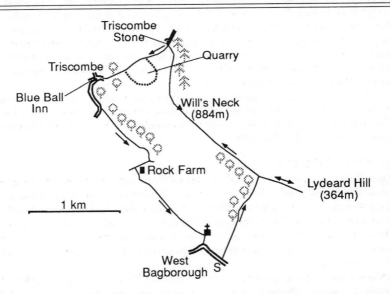

Take the stony path to the left of The Rising Sun Inn and follow it as it rises steeply up on to the Quantocks. This is a fierce climb, its only compensations being the fine stands of beech trees, and the knowledge that almost all of the route's climbing will have been accomplished when it is over. At the top of the path there is a gate. Go through this to reach the Quantock ridge path linking Will's Neck to **Lydeard Hill**. The latter peak is not on the route, but it is certainly worth the short climb, so go right to reach the summit.

From Lydeard Hill go back along the ridge path, passing the gate, to the left, and continue to the top of Will's Neck (*see* Note to Walk 70). From the top head northward to reach the edge of the forest and turn left along it to reach the road and car park, and the Triscombe Stone (*see* Note to Walk 70). From the car park head south-west on a track that goes along the edge of Triscombe Quarry, a huge quarry that takes a very big bite out of the Quantock ridge. Follow the track all the way to the hill base reaching a road close to the Blue Ball Inn.

To continue the route, take the lane that runs to the left of the inn – as you approach it. This lane is unfenced on its left side, and after about 400 yards it is easy to go up through the roadside trees to reach a path contouring around the base of Will's Neck. The path is signed for Rock Farm, and soon reaches a lane (to the right) that goes down to the farm. Turn down this and pass to the right of the farm. Just beyond the farm go left through a kissing gate and follow the clear path beyond across several fields to reach West Bagborough church. Bear right at the church on a path that soon reaches a road. Turn left to return to the centre of **West Bagborough** and the start of the walk.

POINTS OF INTEREST:

Lydeard Hill – The hill is the second highest point on the Quantocks, at 1,194 feet (364 metres). The views from the summit are stunning, with the Brendon Hills, to the west, rising above a fine, broad valley and the Vale of Taunton and Somerset Levels lying to the south and north-east.

West Bagborough – The village church is 15th century and has a fine rood screen. The excellent stained glass dates from the 1920s and was the work of Sir Ninion Camper. Beside the church is Bagborough House an elegant Georgian manor.

REFRESHMENTS:

The Rising Sun, West Bagborough.
The Blue Ball Inn, Triscombe.

Walk 51   **NORTHERN QUANTOCK**   5m (8km)

Maps: OS Sheets Landranger 181; Pathfinder ST 04/14.
A walk that includes the best Quantock viewpoints.
Start: At 117411, the Staple car park.

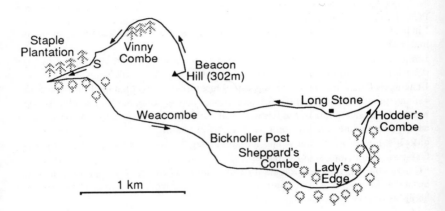

The car park is reached by taking the Bicknoller road out of West Quantoxhead – take
the first turning left after the Windmill Inn when going west – then go first left again.

From the car park take the path south-west towards Weacombe. The path goes
down through the Staple plantation to reach Weacombe Combe. Go left on the path
up the combe to reach Bicknoller Post, a parish boundary marker. Ignore the main
crossing track and head south-east on the path into Sheppard's Combe. Follow the
path between the wooded Lady's Edge and Black Ball wood for $1\frac{1}{4}$ miles (2km) to
reach Hodder's Combe. Where the stream in the combe executes a noticeable S-bend,
use the ford to reach the far bank and a path that climbs steeply up through the woodland
to reach open ground.

Follow the path until a clump of **fir trees** comes into view. There take the left
path (which heads south-west) that climbs up the ridge of Longstone Hill. The

Long Stone for which the path is named is reached by taking the right fork at a Y-junction. Beyond the stone leave the track for a path that heads directly to the Great Road, as the ridge top path is called. At a junction of tracks go north-west to **Beacon Hill**. From the summit return to the main track and head north. Ignore a path that goes south of the Vinny Combe plantation to reach one that goes north of it, and head down into the combe. As the stream in the combe swings right, look for a steep track among the rhododendrons on the far bank, and take this to return to the car park.

POINTS OF INTEREST:

Fir trees – This clump of trees was planted in 1946 as a memorial to local men who had died in the 1939–45 War.

Long Stone – The stone now serves as a parish boundary marker, but is much older, probably dating from the time of the megalith builders, that is the Bronze Age.

Beacon Hill – Even though it is only 1,019 feet (302 metres) high the hill is a superb vantage point. Northward is the Bristol Channel and, beyond, the Welsh hills. To the west are the high moors of the Exmoor National Park. On the coast to the north-east are the cubes of the Hinkley Point Nuclear Power Station. The twin blue cubes are the older, Magnox, 'A' station, while the grey, irregular cube, is the newer Advanced Gas-cooled Reactor (AGR) station.

Beacon Hill is clearly named for its use as a signed fire point, yet local legend has it that when King Alfred camped on the Quantocks while persuing a Danish army, he lit his beacon fire on Longstone Hill.

REFRESHMENTS:

None on route, but the Windmill Inn, West Quantoxhead is only a few minutes away.

Walk 52   **ASH PRIORS**   5m (8km)

Maps: OS Sheets Landranger 181; Pathfinder ST 02/12 and ST 03/13.

Delightful walking in the Vale of Taunton Deane.

Start: At 150290, a lay-by on Ash Priors Common.

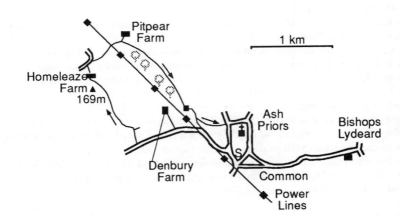

To reach the start turn left off the A358 where a turn right goes to Bishops Lydeard. Go past the **railway station** to reach Ash Priors Common. Ignore a right turn and continue to the junction of four roads. Take the second turning right – the one in the same direction as the power lines – and park in the lay-by a few yards along on the right-hand side.

From the lay-by continue along the road bearing left at a junction. Continue to follow the power lines, but bear left away from them when the road swings left. Walk past the entrance to Kerdon Farm, to the right, and continue for another 500 yards to reach a track, also on the right. Where the track forks, take the left fork into woodland. To the right here are the remains of an old lime kiln. Go past the ruins and follow the track, ignoring all turnings, to reach a **trig point** on the left.

Beyond the trig point bear right through Homeleate Farm and walk down to a road. Go right, passing Down House, to where the road bends left. Here go straight on, following a lane under the power lines towards Pitpear Farm. Before the farm is reached, at the point where the lane swings left towards it, go through the gate ahead and cross the field beyond to reach another gate. Go through and follow the path along the right side of the field beyond. Now follow the wood edge – the path lying between the trees and a stream – and cross a field to reach Denbury Farm. Bear left through the farm to reach the farm lane and follow this around a right-hand bend. About 100 yards beyond the bend go left on a path through woodland. Where the path emerges from the wood bear left and cross two fields to reach a gate on to a road at a T-junction. Go straight ahead on the road into the village of **Ash Priors**, bearing right, with the road, past the church and following it to the Common. At the Y-junction take the right fork down to the junction beneath the power lines. Turn right to return to the lay-by.

POINTS OF INTEREST:

Railway Station – The station (Bishops Lydeard Station) is on the West Somerset Railway, a line that was revived by enthusiasts after British Rail had axed it. The private company that runs the line now operates steam and diesel trains during summer months on a scheduled service from Taunton to Minehead. It would be possible to do the walk here using the station as a start point, adding only 2 miles (3km) to the distance and a truly romantic method of transport to the start.

Trig Point – The correct term for these distinctive white concrete pillars is triangulation point. They were used by the Ordnance Survey to create accurate contour maps of Britain, and were usually placed on hill tops. It is unusual to see one so close to a road and in such a low lying area, yet this small hillock, at 554 feet (169 metres) is a local high spot, as the excellent view towards the Quantocks testifies.

Ash Priors – The church in this delightfully named hamlet is 15th century, but was very heavily restored in Victorian times. The tower is especially attractive.

REFRESHMENTS:

None on the route, but Ash Priors is mid-way between –
The New Inn, Halse – to the south.
The Farmers Arms, Combe Florey – to the north.
and there are several possibilities in Bishops Lydeard.

Walk 53   **DUNDRY HILL**   5m (8km)

Maps: OS Sheets Landranger 172; Pathfinder ST 46/56.

A walk with wonderful views.

Start: At 557669, the car park near Dundry Church.

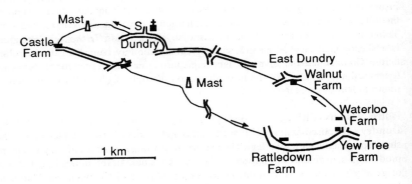

Go through the gate in the car park and head towards the radio masts. Beyond the second mast a stone stile in the field corner gives access to a path down to Castle Farm. Go through the farmyard to emerge on the farm lane. Turn left and follow the lane down to a minor road. Turn left along the road. Ignore a turning on the right to reach a huddle of new houses. Take the rough lane that leads south-east between them, heading for another transmitter mast. In this section of the walk there are tremendous views southward towards Chew Valley lake and the Mendip Hills.

Stay close to the field hedge to pass the mast. Go through a gap in the hedge and follow another hedge across the fields to reach a road. In the last stages two new houses give the line to the road. Cross the road and go slightly right to reach a gate into a field. Cross this by staying close to the left hedge, and cross three more in a similar way. Exit from the last on to a lane and turn right. Follow the lane around a sharp left bend, passing the superb Rattledown Farm and continuing to the hamlet of North Wick.

Just beyond Yew Tree Farm turn left on a farm lane to Waterloo Farm. Go through the farmyard and follow the path beyond which crosses a small stream by way of a stone footbridge. In the field beyond take the path to the left, passing below a series of sheds in which turkeys are reared. The path leads straightforwardly to Walnut Farm on the outskirts of the village of East Dundry.

Go left down Spring Lane to reach a path, to the right, that leads to Spring Farm. From here a path crosses the hillside above the roofs of village houses, then climbs the hill past two prominent trees. Go through a gap in the hedge ahead to reach a road. Turn left and follow the road (Crabtree Lane) to a cross-roads. To the right here there is a phenomenal view of Bristol, virtually the whole city being laid out map-like below. Go over at the cross-roads, ignoring a turn to the right in favour of following Crabtree Lane again. Take the next turning on the right, Church Road, in order to return to **Dundry** and the start of the walk.

POINTS OF INTEREST:

Dundry – Exposed Dundry Hill seems an unlikely place for a village, despite the superb panoramic views it offers. The reason for its siting was stone, the local quarries producing an excellent building stone. The church is built of the stone, though it was originally sited here as a landmark for sailors in Bristol Channel, the Merchant Venturers having built it in the late 15th century.

REFRESHMENTS:
The Dundry Inn, Church Road, Dundry.

Walks 54 & 55   **BADMINTON**   5m (8km) or 10m (16km)
Maps: OS Sheets Landranger 173; Pathfinder ST 88/98.
Two walks around the famous Badminton Estates.
Start: At 804828, in the main street of Great Badminton.

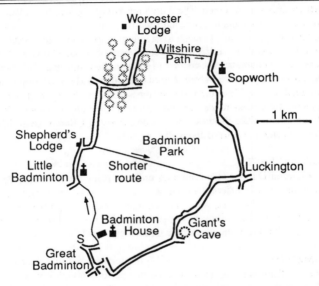

Go east along the main street of **Great Badminton** to reach the gates to the House.
There is a Strictly Private notice on the gates. You will see several more of these on
the route: they refer only to cars, though there is nothing on the sign to tell you this.

From the gates our route heads north up the road marked 'Authorised Vehicles
Only', the road being a pedestrian right of way to Little Badminton. This section of
the walk traverses Badminton Park, an old deer park where the very lucky walker
may still see deer. The walker will also see the kennels of the Beaufort Hunt and will
obtain a different view of Badminton House.

When the road in **Little Badminton** is reached go through the village, continuing
until Shepherd's Lodge is reached on the left. Go right here, following the road to
where it bends sharp left.

At this point the short walk leaves the road, the walker continuing in the same direction as the road section he has just walked, following a track signed as being Private, but adding No Entry to Unauthorised Vehicles. Look left after about 500 yards to see the Great Avenue of woodland that leads to distant Worcester Lodge. After another 700 yards, the walker leaves Avon, temporarily, to do some walking in Wiltshire. A lane is soon reached, near Cherry Orchard Cottage: follow the lane for about 1 mile to reach a road junction and the longer route.

The longer route turns sharp left with the road and follows it along a straight 1 mile section to reach a T-junction. Hidden in the copse across the road here is the Ragged Castle, a folly. Turn right, following the new road across the Great Avenue. About 150 yards beyond the Avenue turn left on a road through Bullpark Wood. When the road emerges from the woods Worcester Lodge can be seen. About 100 yards beyond the trees turn right through a gate to reach the Wiltshire Path, which runs parallel to the wood edge. Follow the path to Sopworth. Turn right on reaching the village, and go across at the road junction, taking the road to Luckington. Turn right as you enter the village, on a road signed for Cherry Orchard. After 400 yards you join the short walk at a road junction near a stone barn.

Now go south, passing Allengrove Farm and eventually reaching another road junction. Turn left and follow the road back to the start in Great Badminton, bearing right at one point so as to follow the estate boundary.

POINTS OF INTEREST:

Great Badminton – The village, which is exquisitely beautiful, is really a dormitory for estate workers, local life centring on Badminton House. The estate was held originally by Henry Somerset, Marquis of Worcester who became the first Duke of Beaufort in 1682. The House dates from the same period, though it was extended by William Kent in the early 18th century. Kent was also responsible for Worcester Lodge and the follies. The 15,000 acre park was landscaped by Capability Brown.

The game of badminton is said to have been invented in the House – literally, when a Duke sought an alternative to the tennis balls which were breaking his windows! – while today the Three-Day Event is one of the world's foremost equestrian events.

The village church, which lies within the estate, has a number of fine memorials including one by Grinling Gibbons, to the first Duke, which is over 25 feet high. Gibbons was also responsible for some beautiful limewood carvings in the House. **Little Badminton** – The village is equally as good as its bigger neighbour, and has a green with a medieval dovecote, and a fine church.

REFRESHMENTS:
The Old Royal Ship, Luckington.

Maps: OS Sheets Landranger 181; Pathfinder SS 84/94.

A walk around the 'typical English village'.

Start: At 992439, the car park at the northern end of Dunster.

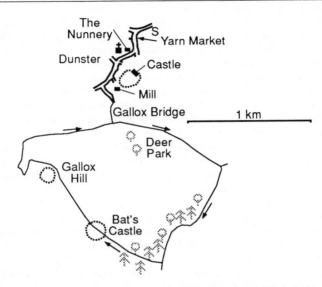

From the car park head down the road past the Exmoor National Park Office to reach **Dunster** High Street. Walk down it, passing the Yarn Market, to the right, and aiming for the castle. At the bottom go right into Church Street passing the Nunnery and the church to the right. Bear left into West Street and take the second turn to the left (Park Street) to reach **Gallox Bridge**. Go over the bridge and at a junction of paths go left over a stile (signed for Carhampton). Follow the rising path through the Deer Park, going through a gate to reach another on to a broad track. Go right, following the sign for Withycombe. After about 800 yards go through a gate in the wall to the right and follow the path over **Bat's Castle** to reach Gallox Hill. The path does not go to the summit of this second hill, crossing its flank to reach woodland.

At a fence with a gate go left, then immediately right through a gap on to a path.

Go left, then right on to a waymarked path that is followed all the way to Gallox Bridge. Now reverse the outward route to the car park.

POINTS OF INTEREST:
Dunster – Dunster is a strong candidate for the typical English village, having all the right ingredients – castle, old tower on a hill, neat church, architectural curios and an old mill. The Yarn Market in High Street is an old cloth market. It was built in the 17th century and damaged in the Civil War, some of the huge timbers still showing the marks of being struck by a cannonball. Dunster Castle was started in Norman times, though there was a previous Saxon building and, probably, a Celtic one before that. Of the Norman castle only a tower and part of a wall remain, the rest being 13th century, with later additions that made it more of a home and less of a fortress. During the Civil War it was held initially by Parliament against a Royalist army, and later by Royalists against a Parliamentarian force. The Prince of Wales, later Charles II, stayed here in 1645.

The Nunnery in Church Street is a beautiful triple-storey, double overhang building, which, despite the name, was never a nunnery, though it was once a guest house for Cleeve Abbey. Quite why it is so-called is a mystery. The church of St George is well worth a visit to see, especially, the 50 foot (16 metre) rood screen, one of the largest in Britain. The screen was made locally and erected in 1499.

To complete the picture, the tower on the hill is Conyger Tower, a folly in the grand style from the late 18th century, and the old mill – Dunster Mill reached along Mill Lane, passed on the walk – is a 17th century corn mill powered, unusually, by two overshot waterwheels.
Gallox Bridge – This medieval pack-horse bridge was called Doddesbridge until the hill above changed its name (see below).
Bat's Castle – An Iron Age hillfort of $3^1/_2$ acres covers the top of this hill.
Gallox Hill – It is believed that the name is a corruption of gallows. Local legend has it that after Monmouth's rebellion and Judge Jeffery's Bloody Assize a gallows was erected on the hill so that local rebels could be executed. Gallox Hill is also topped by a (smaller) hill fort.

REFRESHMENTS:
There are possibilities ranging from simple tea houses to grand restaurants in Dunster.

Walk 57   **WINSFORD HILL**   5m (8km)

Maps: OS Sheets Landranger 181; Pathfinder SS 83/93.
A walk that combines wooded valley and open moor.
Start: At 889335, the Caratacus Stone.

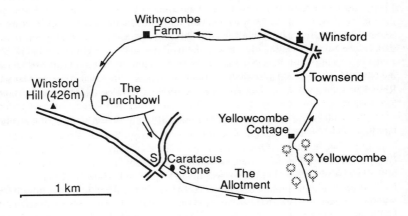

The stone is not at the roadside, but a hundred yards or so to the east of the junction of the B3223 (Exford to Dulverton road) and the minor road which links Winsford to Liscombe and Tarr Steps. There are numerous parking places on the verges of these unfenced roads close to the junction. Use one of these and cross to the stone.

From **Caratacus Stone** follow the path that heads south of east along the line of an old hedge to reach, after about 200 yards, a gate on the left. Go through and turn right to continue in the same direction, passing to the south of a section of common land known as The Allotment. Beyond a clump of trees on the right a gate is reached, also on the right. Ignore this, continuing in the same direction to reach a track coming in from the left. Go through either of two gates ahead and then follow the field edge to reach an old quarry. Just beyond, there is a gate with a yellow waymarker to the left. Go through and follow the path through wooded Yellowcombe.

When Yellowcombe Cottage is seen to the left, leave the main path on a narrow path to the left which goes steeply down to reach a gate. Go through, cross the stream and go through another gate to reach the enclosed Yellowcombe Lane and follow it to reach a road at Townsend. Go right into **Winsford**. At a T-junction in the village go left along Ash Lane, passing the church to the right. About 350 yards beyond the church a path to the left is signed for Winsford Hill via the Punchbowl. Take this, following the yellow waymarked path across several fields, using stiles and gates to cross between them, to reach Withycombe Farm.

The route is well waymarked around the farm, taking the walker over Winn Brook and then right, through a gate, and left, through another, to reach a clear path that climbs up the western edge of **The Punchbowl**. To the right at the top of The Punchbowl is the actual trig point top of Winsford Hill, the summit lying close to the B3223 road. The walk only visits the summit as a detour, continuing along an eastward track that runs away from The Punchbowl. Another track joins from the right, and you start to go downhill towards Winsford (north-east). Here take a narrow path on the right which goes south-east to reach a road. Turn right on this to regain the junction near Caratacus Stone.

POINTS OF INTEREST:

Caratacus Stone – The stone is a real enigma. As a standing stone it could be assumed to be Neolithic or Bronze Age, that is 4,000–6,000 years old, but it is inscribed *Carataci Nepus*, meaning Kinsmen of Caratacus. Now Caratacus was a 1st century AD Celtic warrior who led the Celts of South Wales against the Roman invaders. So why a stone here on Exmoor? and why is the inscription in 5th century Latin? Why, also, does the inscription face away from the track? Has the stone been moved, was it carved after it had been raised? We will never know.

Winsford – The village, whose name is pronounced 'Wince-ford', was the birthplace of Ernest Bevin.

The Punchbowl – Legend has it that the Devil dug the Punchbowl, a spadeful of earth thrown over his shoulder forming Dunkery Beacon. When he wanted to rest the Devil sunbathed by laying across Tarr Steps.

REFRESHMENTS:
The Royal Oak, Winsford.

Walk 58   **CASTLE CARY**   5m (8km)

Maps: OS Sheets Landranger 183; Pathfinder ST 63/73.

To an old railway by way of an older path.

Start: At 641324, the car park in Castle Cary.

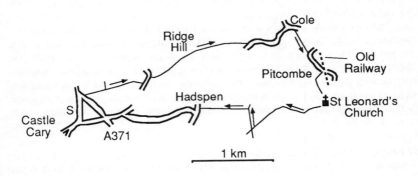

To reach the car park, which is in Catherine's Close, turn into Castle Cary from the A371 opposite the Waggon and Horses and follow the signs.

From the car park turn right into Catherine's Close and turn left to reach traffic lights. Turn right on to the main road, but cross almost immediately and take the bridlepath between Farm House and Combe Lodge. Follow the bridlepath, ignoring a track joining from the left, to reach a road. Turn left and walk to a gap in the hedge on the right. Turn through the gap on to a footpath signed for Cole. Walk along the right-hand hedge to reach a stile. Go over and bear left, then right, to follow the path along the aptly named **Ridge Hill**.

At the end of the ridge the path descends to reach a stile into an orchard. Go over and follow the hedge to the left until it bends away. There turn right and cross the orchard to reach a footbridge. Go over the bridge and turn left to a stile. Go over and turn half-right across the field beyond to reach a stile beside a gate. Go through, or over, on to a road. Turn left into the village of Cole, bearing right where a road joins from the left.

Beyond the last house there is a signed path, for Pitcombe, to the right. Take this, but after a dozen or so steps go over a stile on the right to reach an enclosed path. Follow this to a stile, go over and cross the field to reach a stile to the right of a house. Go over on to a road. Turn right along the road to reach the village of Pitcombe. When the **railway bridge** is reached go right along a lane to reach a stile on the left. Go over and follow the path signed for the church. Two further stiles are crossed before the church is reached.

From the church turn right into a lane. Go through a gate and continue to reach a stile on the right. Go over and half-left across a field to reach a stile. Go over on to a track and turn left along it. At cross-tracks go right, and then take a track to the left about 250 yards further on. Follow the new track to the road in Hadspen. Turn left, then bear right on a road for **Castle Cary**. Follow the road, bearing left at a junction to reach the main A371 at the Waggon and Horses Inn. Cross the road and go down North Street to reach Ansford Road, to the right. Turn up Ansford Road, then go left to reach the car park.

POINTS OF INTEREST:

Ridge Hill – The path along the ridge is an ancient one, dating back to the times when the valley of the River Brue below would have been an inhospitable place.

Railway Bridge – The bridge carried the old Somerset and Dorset railway, still spoken of as the S & D by nostalgic lovers of the days of steam.

Castle Cary – The castle of the name stood on the hill to the south of North Street, but seems to have disappeared by the end of the 12th century. Also gone is the manor house where Charles II spent a night while fleeing south from the disastrous Battle of Worcester. In medieval times the town was famous as a spinning and weaving centre, its speciality being a cloth known as Cary Coarse, valued for its durability. Later sailcloth and linen were made here, and there is still a small rope works.

REFRESHMENTS:

The Waggon and Horses, Ansford.
The White Hart, Fore Street, Castle Cary.
The Countryman, South Street, Castle Cary.

Walk 59 **THE POLDEN HILLS** 5m (8km)

Maps: OS Sheets Landranger 182; Pathfinder ST 42/52 and ST 62/72.

The fine walk above the Somerset Levels.

Start: At 399369, Moorlinch church.

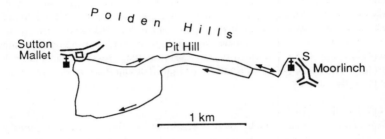

From the church take the path to the bottom right corner of the churchyard where there is a kissing gate. Go through and walk along the field edge to reach a bridlepath. Turn right along the path for 400 yards to reach an enclosed footpath to the left. Take this and follow it for 1 mile (1$^1/_2$ kms) – going sharply right after 100 yards, and equally sharply left after a further $^3/_4$ mile (1,200 metres) – to where it ends in a field. Bear right across this field, going to the left of a telegraph pole to reach another field. Cross this one to its top left-hand corner to reach a track. Turn right along this **old drove road**.

The track heads west, but after another track has joined from the left, it turns sharp right (north). Turn with it, following it into the village of Sutton Mallet. The track passes Sutton Mallet church to reach a road. Go right to reach Nino's Farm, to the right. Here the road bears left: go straight on along an enclosed bridlepath that goes across Pit Hill, one of the **Polden Hills**, towards Moorlinch. The outward journey follows a short section of this path. Where that point is reached follow the outward route back to the church in Moorlinch.

POINTS OF INTEREST:

Old Drove Road – In the days before refrigeration animals were delivered fresh to market by being herded from the farms on which they had been reared all the way to the slaughterhouses of major towns and cities. The routes these animals followed were known as Drove Roads. Along the routes little cottage industries grew up: bulls needed shoeing along the way – as an aside, the shoeing of a bull was reckoned to be one of the most dangerous of country crafts – butchers would kill animals for local villages, and there would be a good supply of inns. The inns did especially good business as the drovers returned with their pockets full of cash. Not only cows and sheep, but pigs and even geese and chickens were herded. The birds had flight feathers removed and their feet dipped in tar to harden them for the walk. Our route follows a section of old drove, with superb views out across Sedgemoor.

Polden Hills – It is said that when Joseph of Aramathea made his journey to Glastonbury he landed at Combwich and followed the ridge top path across the Poldens, probably taking the same path as our route. To the north of our route, at Edington, Alfred the Great fought the battle of Ethandun against the Danes, winning decisively. Alfred moved to the site from his moorland fortress of Athelney (see Walk 77).

REFRESHMENTS:
The Ring O'Bells, Moorlinch.

Walks 60 & 61 **THE DOONE VALLEY** 5m (8km) or 8m (13km)
Maps: OS Sheets Landranger 180 and 181; Pathfinder SS 64/74
and SS 84/94.
In the footsteps of Lorna Doone.
Start: At 792478, the car park, Lorna Doone Farm, Malmsmead.

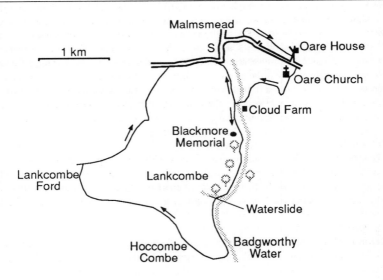

Go over the pack-horse bridge - or through the ford if you wish to try the waterproofing of your boots – and walk along the road to reach Parsonage Farm and Riding Centre to the left. Go down past the farm and turn right over a footbridge. Bear right to a gate and follow the path beyond along the valley, going through several more gates to reach a road near **Oare House**. Go right to a T-junction. Go left to **Oare Church**. Just beyond the church a signed bridleway goes through a gate to the right. Take this, follow the line of the right-hand hedge to another gate. Cross a field to another gate and follow the path beyond around the head of a small combe. Go through a gate and follow the hedge to the right to some sheep pens. Go through these to reach a footpath to Cloud Farm, going under a barn. Go right before the farmhouse to reach a footbridge and go over this on to a track. The short walk returns along this track after visiting the

Blackmore Memorial and waterfall.

Go left on the track, soon passing the **Blackmore Memorial**. Beyond, the path lies close to Badgworthy Water, going into, and out of, a small oak copse to reach a footbridge over the Lank Combe stream. Go over the bridge and go right up the stream for 30 yards to reach the **waterfall**. The short walk returns from here following Badgworthy Water back to Cloud Farm, then continuing along the track, but bearing left away from the stream to reach a road. Go right to return to Lorna Doone Farm.

The longer route continues along Badgworthy Water to reach Hoccombe Combe where a sign points out the path, to the right, for Brendon Common. The old ruins about 100 yards up this path are all that remain of a medieval village. The path climbs to a wall gate, then continues across the Common to reach Lankcombe ford. Here there are many paths: take the one to the right signed for Malmsmead. After about 800 yards take the left fork where the path splits into three indistinct paths. Where this path splits go left again. Ford a stream and follow the path to a road. Go right and follow the road back to the start point.

POINTS OF INTEREST:

Oare House – In *Lorna Doone* this was Plover's Barrow Farm, John Ridd's farm.

Oare Church – Here Carver Doone shot Lorna Doone on her wedding day. The church has been extended since the time of the Doones, so the window marked as being the one Carver shot through, would at that time have overlooked the altar. However, it does not say in the book that the shot was through a window, so perhaps Carver fired from the back of the church.

Blackmore Memorial – Richard Doddridge Blackmore was born in 1825, son of a Berkshire curate, but was brought up by his grandparents after the death of his mother when he was only three months old. Grandfather Blackmore was rector of Oare church and so the boy grew up close to the legend of Lorna Doone. Blackmore became a barrister, but gave it up to write full-time. *Lorna Doone* was his best-selling, and is his most famous, book. The Doone legend has a basis in fact, a group of Scottish outlaws called Doone actually living in Larkcombe in the early 17th century. John Ridd was also a real man, a local farmer and wrestling champion.

Waterfall – In the book John Ridd climbs a waterfall to reach the secret lair of the Doones. The real waterfall is more of a waterslide and does not seem to be the formidable barrier mentioned in the story.

REFRESHMENTS:

There are tea shops in Malmsmead in summer, and Cloud Farm does an excellent ploughman's.

Maps: OS Sheets Landranger 181; Pathfinder SS 84/94.
A walk to Exmoor's heart.
Start: At 837432, Alderman's Barrow.

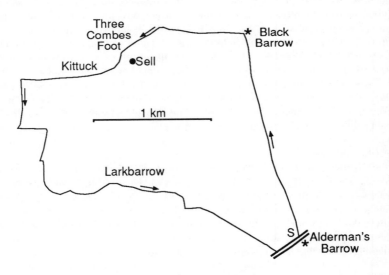

To reach the start take the minor road along the River Exe from Exford – towards Porlock – following it as it climbs and descends Exford Common to reach Lucott Cross. Go left here. **Alderman's Barrow** is about 1 mile (1½km) along on the left-hand side. There is further parking near the cattle grid about 200 yards further on.

Note: This walk is remote and crosses difficult ground. If the walker gets off route he could become lost if visibility is poor. If you are inexperienced in the use of map and compass, and in moorland walking do not attempt the walk in poor weather.

Go through the gate opposite and turn right along the wall to reach a memorial to Major Hilary Cox and his sister. From there an indistinct path heads just west of north all the way to Black Barrow. The walking here is difficult, with rough ground, heather, tussock grass and bracken, and the correct path can sometimes become confused with cross tracks, mostly sheep tracks. To assist, there are boundary stones every few hundred yards, but a map and compass are better insurance.

Black Barrow, another Bronze Age burial mound, lies beside a wall that runs from east to west, but makes a sharp turn northward at the barrow itself. From here the walking is more straightforward as it follows boundaries and clear paths. Go left (west) along the wall reached at Black Barrow. After 400 yards a wall corner is reached: go through the gate on the right, turn left and continue westward, now on the far side of the wall. Soon a gate is reached in the wall. Go through this, following the signed path for Three Combes Foot. The path descends to reach the junction of three streams in a very pretty hollow. To the south is a clump of tall trees. This is a **sell**.

Go over a footbridge and take the signed path (for Larkbarrow) that heads south, then swings right (west) to cross Kittuck. Kittuck is from Kite Oak, one of many boundary trees planted in James I's time. The walking is rough again now, with the path a little indistinct at times, but after gaining the top of Kittuck the next objective, a north-south fence, is clear ahead. Walk to the gate in the fence, go through and turn left (south) along it, to reach a corner. Go over the stile and follow the signed (Larkbarrow Boundary Walk) path on the far side, going east to reach another fence corner and turning right (south) there to reach a wide, easy track. Turn left along this track to reach the ruins of **Larkbarrow**. Continue along the track, with a fence on the right, until a fence corner is reached. Go right through a gate and follow the fence, now on the left, southward. After 100 yards go through a gate in the fence and follow the clear path beyond across the moor to arrive at the road near to the cattle grid alternative start. Go left to return to Alderman's Barrow.

POINTS OF INTEREST:

Alderman's Barrow – The name does not refer to any council official, but is a corruption of Osmund, a Saxon who held land here and at Culbone to the north. The mound is a Bronze Age round barrow.

Sell – Sell is the Exmoor name for a circle of trees placed as a windbreak inside which sheep shelter to avoid being buried by drifting snow.

Larkbarrow – This was a major Exmoor farm – as the extensive ruins suggest – but was taken over in the early 1940s as an army training ground. The training destroyed the farm and it was never resettled.

REFRESHMENTS:

Nothing on the route, though Three Combes Foot is an excellent spot for a picnic, but there is a café and an inn in Exford.

Walk 63   GOBLIN AND BROCKLEY COMBES   5½m (9km)

Maps: OS Sheets Landranger 172; Pathfinder ST 46/56.
A walk through two beautiful wooded combes.
Start: At 456656, the Lord Nelson Inn, Cleeve.

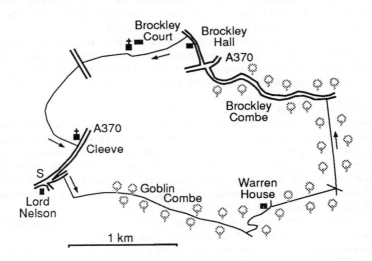

Beside the Lord Nelson there is a lane into which another lane runs, close to the main road. Take this second lane, which runs behind the garage, and then go over a stile on the right into a field. Cross the field to emerge, through a gate, into a rough lane. Turn left and follow the lane beside the high wall of a house to reach the entrance to the beautifully wooded **Goblin Combe**. Take the path through the combe, going through the Nature Reserve to reach a stony path on the left near a Reserve sign. The path leads to more open, but still excellent, ground. Continue to a gate and stile, beyond which is **Warren House**.

To continue, take the third track on the right – the one bearing 67½° (ENE). The tracks traverse Brockley Wood and there are a number of them, many reaching Warren House. Take heart: if you head north you are bound to reach the Brockley Combe road! Follow the ENE path for about 500 yards to reach a junction of tracks. Now take the second track to the left, which leads due north to reach **Brockley Combe** and the road. Turn left and follow the road – but walking parallel to it within the woods – to its junction with the main Bristol-Weston road, the A370. Cross the road and take the lane opposite towards Chelvey and Nailsea. The wall on the left encloses the gardens of Brockley Hall. Just beyond the Hall's lodge a stile on the left leads to a field. Cross this and the field beyond to reach a lane that leads to **Brockley Court** and church. Cross the lane to reach another stile, and cross three fields, each with a stile, to reach a lane.

Cross the lane to a stile. Go over and cross two fields. In the third field head for the gate about halfway along the left edge. Go through and cross a field, heading to the right of Cleeve church tower. The field path reaches the A370 about 100 yards to the right of the church. Turn right and walk back to the Lord Nelson.

POINTS OF INTEREST:

Goblin Combe – The Combe is remarkable for being dry. Despite its valley-like slope no streams run along or into it. This lack of surface water does not affect the trees and shrubs which grow so luxuriously that in summer the Combe can seem a dark and gloomy place. On the walk, especially in autumn and winter when there are fewer leaves to block the view, the limestone cliffs on the Combe's northern flank can be seen. Though not very high, these cliffs are steep and are much favoured by local rock climbers.

The Nature Reserve was set up to protect wild flowers and butterflies, and these make a spring or summer walk through the combe a real joy.

Warren House – The house was once inhabited by the men who looked after the rabbits in Wrington Warren, hence the name. It is in a beautiful position, but is very isolated.

Brockley Combe – Brockley is more open than Goblin, but is equally beautiful, despite the road that runs through it.

REFRESHMENTS:
The Lord Nelson, Cleeve.

Walk 64　　　**LOLLOVER HILL**　　　5¹/₂m (9km)

Maps: OS Sheets Landranger 182; Pathfinder ST 43/53.

A tremendous walk on an 'island' in the Somerset Levels.

Start: At 481346, the Marshall's Elm Youth Hostel.

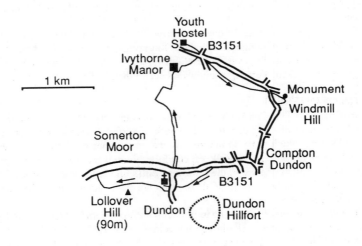

The Youth Hostel is signed off the B3151 about 1¹/₂ miles south of Street.

From the Youth Hostel car park, either walk back along the verge of the untarred road to the B3151, or take the obvious path in the woods to the side (north) of the road to reach the same spot. Cross the B3151 to reach the minor road for Kingweston, but almost immediately go right over a stile on to an indistinct path that climbs up to the ridge of Collard Hill. Go along the ridge, going over several stiles, to reach a track down to a road. Cross the road and follow a path that climbs wooded Windmill Hill to reach the **Monument** in a clearing at the top.

Facing south, take the left-hand path to its junction with a bridlepath. Turn right along the bridlepath to reach a road. Turn left and follow the road for ²/₃ mile (1 kilometre) to reach a junction where the road bends sharply back right. Go with the road to reach another junction in Compton Dundon. Go left and follow the road to its junction with the B3151. Go left, then cross to reach Ham Lane and follow this past a collection of delightful thatched cottages. About 400 yards from the B3151 go left through a signed gate by a lay-by and follow **a church path** on flagstones across a field. The path aims for some barns, going to the right of these and then through a gated farmyard to reach an enclosed path. Cross a field along its left edge to a gate. Go through and cross the field ahead along its right edge to a gate on to a wide path. To the left here is **Dundon Hill**. Go down the path to the road in Dundon village.

Go left then cross to reach a footpath signed for Lollover Hill. This soon joins a wider cross-track. Go right on this and follow it round a sharp left turn. Climb up the flank of **Lollover Hill**, passing the trig point summit. Go through a gate and descend with a hedge on your right. Go over a stile on the right and descend a path to reach a road, Dundon Hayes Lane. Turn right along this and follow it to a cross-roads.

Turn left at the cross-roads, following a metalled lane that soon becomes a green lane. Follow it to its end, then cross a ditch and go through a gate on the left. Turn right, along the ditch, to reach a gate on the right. Go through and cross a field close to its left edge to reach a sleeper bridge and stile. Cross, and follow the left edge of the next field to reach another sleeper bridge and stile. Cross and go right on a track that goes uphill past Ivythorne Manor to reach the B3151. Go left, and left again on the minor road back to the Youth Hostel.

POINTS OF INTEREST:

Monument – The monument is to Sir Samuel Hood who was born in Butleigh, a village to the east, in 1724. The monument has suitable naval inscriptions. From it there is a wonderful view of Glastonbury Tor, to the north.

Church Path – There is no church in Compton Dundon, the villagers walking to Dundon church along a pathway of flagstones so that they could arrive with mud-free boots.

Dundon Hill – The hill is topped by an Iron Age hillfort and forms the head of the Gemini figure in the Zodiac said to be drawn by features around Glastonbury.

Lollover Hill – Though only 295 feet (90 metres) high the hill is an impressive viewpoint. This is due to its position, thrust out westward so that it sits like an island in Somerton Moor.

REFRESHMENTS:

None on route, but there are numerous possibilities in nearby Street.

Walk 65   **HADDON HILL** $5^1/_2$m (9km)

Maps: OS Sheets Landranger 181; Pathfinder SS 82/92.

A river walk that visits Exmoor's largest lake.

Start: At 970285, the Haddon Hill car park.

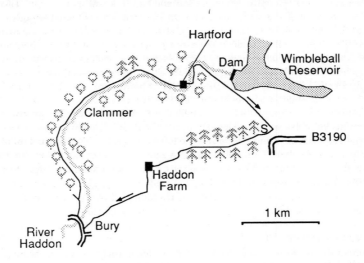

The car park is on the right side of the B3190 which links Ralegh's Cross to Bampton, at the point where the road bends sharp left about $1^1/_2$ miles ($2^1/_2$km) beyond the village of Upton.

    At the far end of the car park there is a fenced forestry plantation. A gate in the fence gives access to a forest road: follow this, ignoring turns to left and right. After about 800 yards the track reaches a gate. Go through and follow the wide path beyond, which leads you in the same direction. Where the forest becomes more mixed (i.e. deciduous trees as well as conifers) the path swings right, continuing to reach a sheep fold at the plantation's edge. Go left here, passing through the last of the trees and follow a hedge, on the right, to a farm lane. Turn right along this lane to Haddon Farm.

    Go past the farm and turn left down on enclosed, overgrown path. Follow this, going around a right bend after about 350 yards. The path ends at a gate. Go through this to reach a short lane past some delightfully named cottages. The lane ends at a road. Turn right to go through the rest of the village of Bury, going over the River Haddon either on the beautiful pack-horse bridge or through the ford. Beyond the river there is a fork where the road goes left and a lane goes right. Follow the lane to reach another fork. Here the lane goes left and uphill, a path going right. Take the path and follow it all the way to the hamlet of Hartford. This is Lady Harriet's Drive, named for Lady Harriet Acland, wife of Col Acland whose family owned many of Exmoor's acres – and who made large and generous gifts of land to the National Trust. The Drive was taken by Lady Harriet's carriage, and hopefully she enjoyed it as much as you will. It is a delightful piece of walking, between the river and the steeply wooded flank of Hartford Bottom. A few houses are passed at Clammer, but then it is nature at her best until Hartford Lodge is reached.

At Hartford the route reaches a metalled lane. Follow this until a signpost for the dam points through a small gate into Hartford Mill. Bear left to the far end of a garden, turn right to reach the River Haddon and go left over a bridge. Turn left and follow the river to a concrete road. Turn right to reach a gate. Go through and follow the road to the dam, staying with the road as it goes up the dam's southern edge, to reach **Wimbleball Reservoir**. Continue along the road, bearing right at a fork and heading away from the reservoir along the flank of **Haddon Hill**. As the road enters a small section of woodland, go right on a signed path back to the car park.

POINTS OF INTEREST:

Wimbleball Reservoir – The reservoir was created in early 1978 after the huge dam – 164 feet (50 metres) high was built across the Haddon Valley. As the reservoir is inside the Exmoor National Park its creation caused great public controversy. The Water Board attempted to allay fears by having it landscaped by Dame Sylvia Crowe, stocking it with trout and opening it as a recreation area. Whether that was, and is, sufficient is for the walker to judge.

Haddon Hill – The hill above the car park can be climbed with a 1 mile ($1^1/_2$km) extension to the walk, following the marked path. The view from the 1,164 foot (355 metre) summit is superb, Dartmoor, the Blackdown Hills – with the Wellington Monument prominent – and Dunkery Beacon all being visible.

REFRESHMENTS:

None on route, though there is a picnic area beside the car park, and the summit of Haddon Hill would also make an excellent picnic site. There is, however, a good range of facilities in nearby Bampton.

Walk 66   **CHEDDAR GORGE**   5¹/₂m (9km)

Maps: OS Sheets Landranger 182; Pathfinder ST 45/55.

A superb walk around the famous Cheddar Gorge.

Start: At 483546, a lay-by on the B3135 near Black Rock Gate.

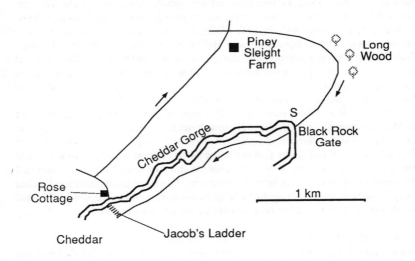

The start point is reached by following the road up Cheddar Gorge. Black Rock Gate is reached to the left just after the last of the Gorge's cliffs have been left behind. The route starts by following the **West Mendip Way**, a waymarker for which, signed for Draycott, lies opposite the lay-by. Follow the marked path which rises steeply through excellent woodland to reach open ground, level with the top of **Cheddar Gorge**. The path goes quite close to edge of the Gorge cliffs: this offers a fine view, but please beware – the cliff edge is unfenced and the drop is, at its highest, 425 feet (130 metres) and virtually sheer to the road.

When the West Mendip Way turns off left stay with the cliff top path until the observation tower and the top of Jacob's Ladder is reached. Descend the 300 steps of the Ladder – there is a small fee in summer time – to the Gorge road. Turn right, and pass a small reservoir, to the left, to reach Rose Cottage. Go left in front of the Cottage to reach a path which passes the drive to a house and then bears right behind a cottage. When another cottage is reached go sharp right on a steep, uphill path.

Follow the path up through woodland, but where it turns go over a stile to the left. Bear right with the path beside an old wall, ignoring all turns to the right. When a stone stile is reached cross it and follow the left edge of fields to reach Piney Sleight Farm. Go to the left of the farmouse and follow the farm lane. After about 300 yards the West Mendip Way is rejoined by crossing a stile to the right. Follow the wall to the right to reach a stile into Long Wood. The Wood is exited over a stile: ignore a left turn – over a stile – which heads off to Velvet Bottom, following the wall instead to reach the Black Rock Quarry. Stay on the main path that runs between the Quarry and the Nature Reserve to the left to reach Black Rock Gate and the start of the walk.

POINTS OF INTEREST:

West Mendip Way – The Way is a continuously waymarked route which traverses the Mendips from Uphill to Wells, a distance of some 30 miles. A local test piece is to complete the walk in one day.

Cheddar Gorge – The Gorge is one of the most dramatic natural features in Britain, a huge cleft in the limestone platform of the southern Mendips, with near vertical cliffs over 400 feet high. The town nestling at the foot of the gorge is famous for its cheese – there is still one cheese-maker operating here – and strawberries. Between the old town and the natural beauty of the high cliffs lies the tourist Gorge, a seemingly endless array of souvenir shops and attractions. Unquestionably the best of these are the show caves of Goughs and Cox's. These caves are important archaeologically for their period of human occupation, but also have spectacularly beautiful stalactite and stalagmite formations.

Black Rock – The Quarry was named for its dark grey limestone. Quarrying was a relatively late industry on the Mendips, early exploitation being for the lead held in the limestone rock matrix. Some historians have claimed that the Romans invaded Britain in order to occupy the Mendip lead mines.

The Black Rock Nature Reserve covers 121 acres and protects the unique limestone flora. The Cheddar Pink (*Diantaus Grationopolitanus*) grows only on the Gorge cliffs, but several species of rare orchids are found in the Reserve.

REFRESHMENTS:

Difficult to miss in lower Cheddar Gorge!

A left turn at the bottom of Jacob's Ladder offers a short detour to Cheddar village where less exuberent refreshments are available. The Butcher's Arms, just a couple of hundred yards away, is expecially good.

Walks 67 & 68 **DUNKERY BEACON** $5\frac{1}{2}$m (90km) or 10m (16km)
Maps: OS Sheets Landranger 181; Pathfinder SS84/94.
Two walks that include the highest point of Exmoor.
Start: At 902439, the Webber's Post car park.

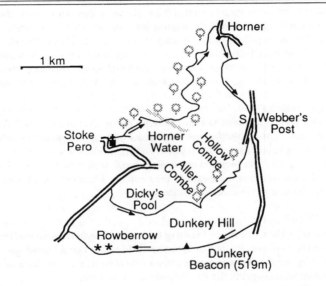

The car park is close to the junction of two roads. Cross to the far one – that which is furthest to the east, and follow its verge up Luccombe Hill to reach, after about $1\frac{1}{4}$ miles (2km) a broad track through the heather to the right. This track heads for the distinctively cairned summit of **Dunkery Beacon** visible on the skyline. After taking in the superb views from the top, take the ridge path westward, passing the barrow of **Rowbarrow** and bearing half-right there down a wide track to reach a road. Go right down the road to reach, after about $\frac{3}{4}$ mile ($1\frac{1}{4}$km), a path to the right, signed as **Dicky's Path**.

   The short walk takes this path which drops down into Bagley Combe, but then contours around the northern flank of Dunkery Hill. Ignore all paths which lead off uphill to the right: these are heading for Dunkery Beacon. The path drops down into the cleft of Aller Combe, rising sharply out of it to continue eastward across open moor. The next cleft is Hollow Combe. Again the path goes downhill, using a footbridge to cross the combe's stream before climbing to emerge on open moor again. Follow the path as it contours around the hill to reach a road. Go right, along this, to regain the car park.

The longer route follows the road verge to reach **Stoke Pero**. Go past the church and turn right beyond the house on a signed track. Go along this to a gate. Go through and follow the path beyond downhill, bearing left once to reach a footbridge over Horner Water. Climb the path beyond (**Granny's Ride**) through Horner Wood. At the top of the climb the path swings leftward, descending as it does. Where it starts to climb again there is a path junction. Take the right fork and follow it as it meanders through a beautiful section of woodland. Eventually the path drops down into the Horner Water valley to reach, to the right, an old pack-horse bridge into Horner. Go over the bridge to reach a road. Turn right and follow the road around a left bend. Pass the last houses in Horner and climb a little to reach a signed path to the right. Take this path which climbs up through woodland to reach a T-junction of paths. Go right and follow the wide track, ignoring all turns to left and right. The track contours around Horner Hill, emerging from the trees on to open moor with views into the Horner Water valley (to the right), and forward to the car park. Follow the track back into trees to emerge back at the Webber's Post car park.

POINTS OF INTEREST:

Dunkery Beacon – The name is said to derive from the Celtic *dun creagh* (rocky hill), which seems a little unlikely in view of the smoothed profile. Local legend has it that the hill topped by the Beacon was created when the Devil threw a spadeful of earth over his shoulder while digging the Punchbowl near Winsford.

Rowbarrow – The barrows here are Bronze Age burial mounds.

Dicky's Path – The path was named by the Acland family, who owned the Horner estate, several of whose members were called Richard.

Stoke Pero – The church here is the highest on Exmoor, and one of the most remote. The name is a mix of Saxon (Stoke = farm) and Norman (Pero from Pirou in Normandy).

Granny's Ride – Another favourite outing of the Aclands. This one, presumably, was named for an elderly member of the family.

REFRESHMENTS:

In season there is a tea shop in Horner. Otherwise there are inns and cafés in nearby Porlock.

Maps: OS Sheets Landranger 181; Pathfinder SS 83/93.
A walk to the high point of the Brendon Hills.
Start: At 931393, the church in Cutcombe.

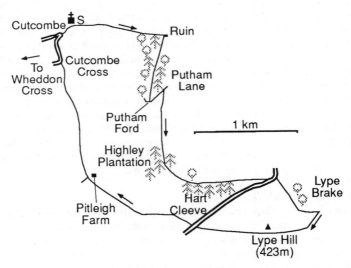

Go down the lane in front of the church and go through the first gate on the right. Go across the field diagonally to reach a stile in the left-hand corner. Go over and cross the next field downhill to a gate. Go through this and continue downhill. Cross several more fields, continuing downhill, to reach the bank of a stream beyond the trees. The last section of the path to the riverbank is somewhat overgrown, but quite obvious. Walk along the bank until a **ruined building** at the water's edge is reached. Go behind this to cross the stream and turn back along the opposite bank for a short while to reach a path that bears left, away from the water.

The path reaches, and follows, another stream through Putham Wood. Continue to reach Putham Lane, bearing left with it to ford the stream at Putham Ford. Walk up the lane for 200 yards to reach a track on the right. Turn on to this track and follow it across several fields to reach the edge of Highly Plantation. Go through the trees to reach a gate. Go through and follow the path down to a stream. Cross the stream and aim for the gap in the line of beeches ahead. Go through and turn left along the line of trees to reach a yellow waymarked stile. Go over and follow the waymarked path to reach a forestry track. The track is signed for Whedden Cross which is confusing as you are walking away from it. No matter: follow the track to a road.

Turn left along the road for 100 yards to reach a yellow waymarked gate on the right – just before a thatched cottage. Go through and follow the path signed for Luxborough. The path is well waymarked, following a hedge to reach the top of wooded Lype Brake. After a building has been passed a gate is reached. Go through and turn right, up the hill. There is no path, but the field edge can be followed. Go through a gate and climb for a further 100 yards to reach a red waymarked gate on the right. Go through and follow the path to the trig point summit of **Lype Hill**.

Continue along the red waymarked path to reach a road. Cross and go through the gate opposite on to a path signed for Wheddon Cross. The path is clear and well waymarked in red, going over several fields to reach Pitleigh Farm. Go to the left of the farm and continue on the red waymarked path, crossing more fields to arrive at a road at Cutcombe Cross. Go ahead, along the road, to return to **Cutcombe**, bearing right at a leftward hairpin bend to reach the church.

POINTS OF INTEREST:

Ruined Building – The ruin is of Stowey Mill, long disused and covered in vegetation, but once the chief watermill in the area. Its presence at this unlikely spot explains the number of paths.

Lype Hill – The hill is the highest point of the Brendon Hills, at 1,387 feet (423 metres), and is an excellent viewpoint. To the east and north-east are the Quantocks, the Somerset Levels and the Mendips. To the north-west is Selworthy Beacon and the Somerset coast, while westward are Dunkery Beacon and Exmoor. Southward the view extends across Devon and Dartmoor.

Cutcombe – There is little enough in this tiny hamlet, but the church is worth a visit. It has a 13th century tower with fine gorgoyles, though the rest is mid-19th century.

REFRESHMENTS:

None on the walk, though the Rest and Be Thankful Inn at Wheddon Cross is only a short distance away.

Walk 70 CROWCOMBE AND WILL'S NECK 5½m (9km)

Maps: OS Sheets Landranger 181; Pathfinder ST 03/13.

A second route to the highest Quantock summit.

Start: At 140366, the Church House car park, Crowcombe.

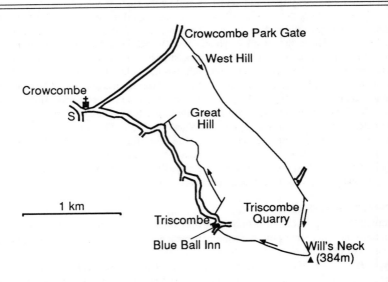

Go through the gap beside Church House to the village road, opposite the church. Go right and take the first turn to the left. Follow the road up Crowcombe Combe to the Quantock ridge top. There go right along the ridge track which goes over West Hill, then along the flank of Great Hill. The section of the ridge track is an old drove road, (*see* Note to Walk 59), and passes some superb beech trees.

Ignore tracks to the right that go down Triscombe Combe and cross the top of a road near a car park. In the car park is the **Triscombe Stone**. Ahead now the old drove road is called **Alfred's Road**: leave it when a clear path heads off half-right to the summit of **Will's Neck**. From the summit go north of west down the ridge to reach the narrow belt of trees at the base of the hill. Go through these to reach a road. Go right to reach the Blue Ball Inn. Go left past the inn, then right into Triscombe, on the road for Crowcombe. Follow the road for 100 yards to reach a track to the right. Go up this to reach a gate. Go through and bear left immediately on a path through woodland that, in autumn, is alive with pheasants. Cross a fence by means of a gate hidden behind a tree to reach the lower slopes of Great Hill. Stay with the path around the hill to reach a track. Go left on the track to reach a road. Go right, and bear right again after 200 yards on a road back to Crowcombe and the start of the walk.

POINTS OF INTEREST:

Triscombe Stone – The stone is only about 2 feet (60 cms) high, but despite its apparent insignificance is the legendary mustering point for the Yeth Hounds, the hounds of death who hunted the Quantock ridge. The hounds are accompanied by ghostly riders and travel at breakneck speed. To see or hear them meant certain death. However, it was said that the hounds only hunted on moonless or stormy nights. Even today many locals will walk miles rather than cross the ridge on such nights - or so it is said.

Alfred's Road – The name derives from the ridge track's use by King Alfred as he sought an invading Danish army.

Will's Neck – The curious name of the Quantocks' highest peak – at 1,260 feet (384 metres) – is Saxon and comes from their word *wallas*, which meant foreigner. At one stage the Quantocks separated the Celts from the Saxons as the latter pushed west across Britain, and the hills were probably named then. The same Saxon word gives us Wales, Valais in Switzerland and Walloon in Belgium.

Crowcombe – The Church House is probably late 15th century and was a church-ale house. Such houses sold food and drink on saint's days and fair days with all profits going to the church. Very few such houses now exist. On your way past look at the hollowed out steps of the external stairway, worn by thousands of feet over hundreds of years. The church opposite the House is late 14th century and has a fine font from that time. In the churchyard there is an old preaching cross, and there is also a 13th century market cross in the village centre.

REFRESHMENTS:
The Blue Ball Inn, Triscombe.
Stable Cottage, Triscombe.
The Carew Arms, Crowcombe.

Walk 71   HORTON COURT   6m (9½km)

Maps: OS Sheets Landranger 172; Pathfinder ST 67/77.

A walk down the Cotswold Edge to one of its most interesting buildings.

Start: At 779870, the centre of Hawkesbury Upton.

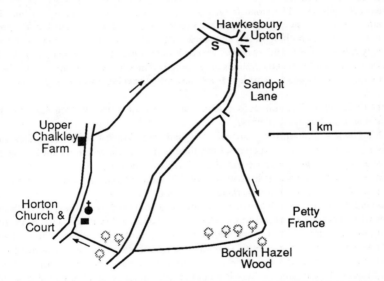

Leave the village southward along Sandpit Lane. After about 500 yards, a wide track leaves the lane half-left. Take this, and at its end cross a field to reach a path along a stone wall. Half-left ahead now can be seen the houses of **Petty France**. The walk does not reach the village, however, going right on a rough track which is reached soon after the wall has turned sharply left. The track goes past the delightfully named Bodkin Hazel Wood and reaches Highfield Lane, a continuation of Sandpit Lane. The Cotswold Way follows Highfield Lane, on the far side. Our route joins the Cotswold Way by crossing the lane and taking the waymarked footpath.

The footpath goes down the wooded Cotswold Edge, emerging on a minor road. To the left from here is Horton village, but we go right to reach the village church and **Horton Court**. After visiting the Court and church continue along the minor road for about 800 yards to reach Upper Chalkley farm, to the left. Opposite the farm's last barn a signed, but somewhat indistinct, path leads off beyond a gate. Cross a field, go through a gate and cross a small stream near a cottage.

Do not follow the stream: instead continue ahead to reach a gate to another field. In this field a track is crossed to reach another gate. The path is more distinct now, and the houses of Hawkesbury Upton also act as a beacon. Cross several more fields to reach a small playing field on the left side of which a short alley leads back to the start in the main village street.

POINTS OF INTEREST:

Petty France – During the early Medieval period Britain exported wool to mainland Europe, particularly the Low Country region, and imported finished woollen cloth. It soon became apparent to the Crown that this did not make economic sense, and it was decided to entice Flemish weavers to Britain in order to set up a rival industry. Many of these weavers were settled in Pembrokeshire to create an 'English' enclave in Wales. Others were settled in the Cotswolds and two local village names, Dunkirk and Petty France (that is *Petit France*), reflect their origins in this settlement. In addition, the church at nearby Little Sodbury is dedicated to St Adeline, the patron saint of Flemish weavers.

Horton Court – The Court has a considerable claim to being the oldest inhabited domestic building in England, its hall having been built in the first half of the 12th century for the Norman Robert du Tedini. As a purely domestic building it is very rare, most of the new Norman lords of the manor taking the precaution of fortifying their houses.

The Court was extended by Dr William Knight in the first quarter of the 16th century. Dr Knight was the son of peasant farmers, but his natural abilities brought him fame and honour as a lawyer. He was chief secretary to Henry VIII and negotiated with the Pope in Rome for his divorce from Katherine of Aragon. Dr Knight was proud of his achievements, most particularly of his coat-of-arms which is displayed over the Court's main door.

The loggia or ambulatory, in the garden was also built by Knight. Its obvious Roman styling is made even more pronounced by the medallions of Roman emperors on the back wall.

REFRESHMENTS:
The Duke of Beaufort Inn, Hawkesbury Upton.

Maps: OS Sheets Landranger 193; Pathfinder ST 01/11 and ST 02/12.
Up the Blackdowns to Wellington's Monument.
Start: At the North Street car park, Wellington.

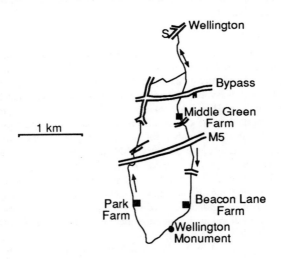

To reach the car park, drive into Wellington from Taunton, go straight on at the traffic lights and turn right 100 yards further on, at the parking sign.

From the car park walk back to Wellington's main street, Fore Street, and turn right. Cross to reach the Three Cups Inn and go under its archway to follow an alleyway on to a road. Go right, then first left to reach a path (Park Lane) that crosses two roads (Wellesley Park and Barn Meads Road) to reach the Wellington bypass. Cross the road, slightly right, to reach a stile. Go over and go half-right across a field to reach another stile. Go over and turn left to follow the hedge to a kissing gate. Cross the field ahead to a gate on to a road.

Cross the road and go up the farm lane ahead. Go through a gate near Middle Green Farm and follow the path to the M5 motorway. Go under the motorway by tunnel and cross three fields, staying close to the hedge to the left in each. The last field leads you to a road: cross and go up the farm lane ahead to reach Beacon Lane Farm. When the farm buildings are reached, go right into a field and cross it to reach a gate. Go through into woodland and follow the path upwards. The last few feet are very steep and steps have been constructed to aid the walker. At the top of the steps is the **Wellington Monument**.

There is a car park to the west of the monument. Walk past this, feeling suitably superior, on a path that goes along the tree line – to be exact just inside the last trees – for 500 yards to reach a gate on to a downhill track. Go through and turn right (downhill), following the track through Park Farm to reach the farm lane. Continue down this, going under the motorway again – where the lane bears right, then left, to reach a T-junction. Go right. Go through the first gate on the left and turn half-right across the field, beyond, keeping to the right of a stream. Go over a low fence and cross the next field to a gate. Go through and turn right along the road to a T-junction. Turn left and walk down to the bypass.

Cross to reach a lane and go along it to reach, on the right, a stile, set just beyond the second house on the right. Cross the field close to the right-hand fence to reach a road. Turn right, the first left into Ardwyn. Follow this slightly uphill to reach the start of Wellesley Park and the outward journey. Turn left along the path and reverse the outward route back to **Wellington**.

POINTS OF INTEREST:

Wellington Monument – The hero of Waterloo had little connection with the Somerset town whose name he took when he was ennobled, it being likely that he chose it because it was close, in sound, to his family name of Wellesley. Nevertheless the townsfolk were overjoyed and in 1817 it was decided to raise a monument to the great man on the Blackdown Hills. The monument, a 175 foot (53 metre) obelisk, now dominates the local skyline. The 235 steps to its top can be climbed – a torch is needed, as is the key, obtainable from Monument Farm, the other side of the car park passed by the walk – for a tremendous view.

Wellington – Relieved of its burden of holiday traffic by a bypass and the M5 motorway, Wellington is now a charming little place with several interesting spots. The Town Museum, in an old country inn in Fore Street, has a good local collection, while the church has an impressive tomb to Sir John Popham, a local man who was the judge at the trials of Walter Raleigh and Guy Fawkes.

REFRESHMENTS:

There are many possibilities in Wellington, but none on the walk.

HAM HILL
6m (9½km)

Maps: OS Sheets Landranger 183 & 193; Pathfinder ST 41/51.
Full of interest from start to finish.
Start: At 479169, The Prince of Wales Inn, Ham Hill Country
Park.

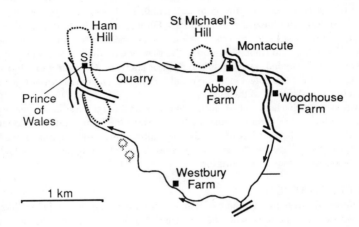

From the Prince of Wales – surely England's only inn lying within the ramparts of an
Iron Age hillfort – follow the clear downhill path beside the hamstones (as the local
quarried output are known), signed for Montacute and East Stoke, bearing left to
reach a track by some blackthorns. Follow the track, leaving it to the left at a sign for
Montacute. Go round a quarry, to the right, to reach a wood. Go down to an old wall
and turn right along it – the wall is on your left hand – following a path that occasionally
crosses the wall. The path reaches a stile: go over and follow the path through the
woods, exiting over another stile. Where the path forks go right to a stile. Go over and
pass below **St Michael's Hill**. Continue along the path to reach **Abbey Farm**. Turn left
along the farm lane to reach the church in **Montacute**.

From the church turn right along the main road to reach The Borough, as the centre of Montacute is called. Continue to reach a garage on the right, and go right, up the lane just beyond it. Pass Woodhouse Farm, to the left, and continue to a junction at the top of the hill. Turn left, and almost immediately left again into a farm lane. Follow the lane for 200 yards, then go left on to an enclosed bridlepath. Follow the bridlepath for 500 yards then go right on to another enclosed bridlepath and follow it for 1 mile ($1\frac{1}{2}$km) going past Westbury Farm. About 500 yards beyond the farm the bridlepath reaches the edge of Norton Covert. Here go right on a path signed for **Ham Hill**.

There is a left turn halfway up the hill: ignore this, continuing to the top of the hill and turning left there on a path below the northern ramparts of Ham hillfort. Stay on the path, ignoring all turns to the right, as it turns northward to join a road. There are car parks to the left and right from here, any of which you might have used. To reach the Prince of Wales, go left and follow the road until a signed road, to the right, is reached.

POINTS OF INTEREST:

St Michael's Hill – The hill can be climbed by a steep path beyond the stile and National Trust plaque. The hill was sacred to the Saxons after Tofig, standard-bearer to Cnut, dug up a cross there. The cross was taken to Essex where Waltham Abbey was built around it. To the mortification of the locals the Normans built a castle on the hill. The tower is an 18th century folly. The Greek inscription above the door means look out, though whether this is a warning or a comment on the panorama from the top is hard to say.

Abbey Farm – This was one of the last buildings to be constructed by the monks of the nearby Cluniac Priory. There are a few remains of the Priory itself, close to Montacute Manse.

Montacute – This pretty little village is most famous for Montacute House one of England's finest Elizabethan houses. The House is now owned by the National Trust and is open to the public from April to October.

Ham Hill – The hillfort on top of the hill is huge, the 3 miles (5km) of its ramparts enclosing over 200 acres. Though Iron Age in origin it was also occupied by the Romans as it overlooked Fosse Way. The quarries extracted Ham stone, the beautiful golden stone of which Monacute is built.

REFRESHMENTS:
The Prince of Wales, Ham Hill.
The King's Arms, Montacute.
The Tudor Rose Tea-Rooms, Montacute.

Walk 74   **FARLEIGH HUNGERFORD CASTLE**   6m (9½km)

Maps: OS Sheets Landranger 172 and 173; Pathfinder ST 65/75 and ST 85/95.

A tremendous walk, with delights all the way.

Start: At 789602, the church in Freshford.

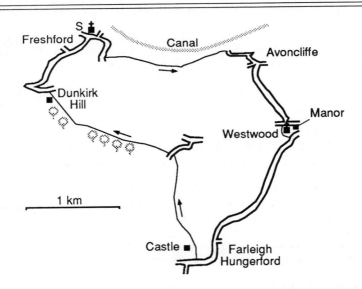

Walk south-east from the church, passing The Inn and going across a bridge over the River Frome. Turn left immediately on a path that heads across a field. The path continues in a superb position, hemmed in by the River Avon to the left and the wooded valley side to the right. Soon the aqueduct, built in 1803, which takes the canal over the Avon – and over the GWR railway – appears ahead. To reach it the walk has to pass into Wiltshire. The high-walled house here was a weaving centre in the 17th century, but served as the area's workhouse in the 19th century. The Cross Guns Inn – across the canal – can be reached from here, though the route does not actually go past it, climbing steeply up to the right instead. At the top of the climb is the village of Avoncliff. Follow the road up to reach the village of Westwood. At a T-junction cross to reach a path that is followed to reach **Westwood church**. To the left of the path is **Westwood Manor**.

Beyond the church follow the path to a road. Go right and follow this quiet road to Farleigh Hungerford crossing back into Somerset on the way. The road goes steeply down to reach the main A366 close to the hamlet. Turn right for 300 yards, then go right again to reach **Farleigh Hungerford Castle**.

From the castle follow the path between it and the River Frome, going past a trout farm and over several fields to reach a lane. Cross and go over the stile opposite to reach a path that stays a little further away from the river. Cross several fields to reach a gate and stile into Friary Wood. The path exits the wood through another gate and uses a precarious plank bridge to cross a stream near a group of cottages. Go over a stile and follow the path to the road at **Dunkirk Mill**. Go left and steeply up the road to reach, after about 250 wearing yards, a Y-junction. Go sharply back right on an easier road that leads back into Freshford. Follow the road, ignoring all turnings, back to the village church.

POINTS OF INTEREST:

Westwood Church – The church has a superb 15th century stained glass east window showing the Crucifixion above a lovingly depicted vase of flowers and an array of wild flowers, a most unusual form.

Westwood Manor – Westwood is a 15th century manor house, but with late 16th century additions and alterations. It has superb Gothic and Jacobean windows and, inside, excellent Jacobean plasterwork. The topiary garden is modern. The Manor is owned by the National Trust and is open from April to September on Tuesday and Wednesday afternoons.

Farleigh Hungerford Castle – The castle was built in the 14th century and though ruinous is of great interest. The chapel is of special note for its wall paintings – look out for the knights in armour – stained glass and the tomb of Sir Thomas Hungerford who built the castle. The castle is in the care of English Heritage, and is open all year: April – September, daily 10am – 6pm, October – March, Tuesday – Sunday 10 am – 4pm.

Dunkirk Mill – The weaving centre at Avoncliff was run by Flemish weavers who probably gave the name Dunkirk to the mill to remind them of home.

REFRESHMENTS:
The Inn, Freshford.
The Cross Guns, near Avoncliff.
The Old Malt House, Westwood.

139

Walk 75   CHEW MAGNA AND STANTON DREW   6m (9¹/₂km)

Maps: OS Sheets Landranger 172; Pathfinder ST 46/56.

A fine village, and an interesting stone circle.

Start: At 577633, the church at Chew Magna.

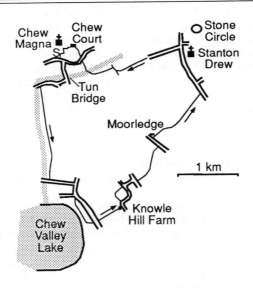

With your back to the church head south, leaving **Chew Magna** along Tunbridge Road. Cross **Tun Bridge** and go right into Dumpers Lane, a cul-de-sac. Where the lane ends follow the footpath on the left over a stile to the River Chew. Follow the path beside the river over several stiles to reach a lane. Turn left along this to reach a road – Denny Lane, a continuation of Tunbridge Road. Go right, following the road to a road junction. On the other side is a car park and picnic area beside Chew Valley Lake.

From the car park a lakeside path leads off to a second car park and picnic area. From there take a path through conifers to reach a road. Cross and turn right along the road verge for 50 yards to reach a gate. Go through and follow a signed path along the left hedge of the field to Knowle Hill Farm. Go through the farmyard to reach a lane. Turn left and follow the lane as it skirts the base of Knowle Hill. The lane bends left around the hill base, then goes right to reach a T-junction. Turn right. After 200 yards, just before the Pony and Trap Inn, go through a signed gate on the left and cross the field beyond to reach a stile in the bottom left-hand corner. Go over and follow the right edge of the next field to a gate. Go through, cross a shallow stream and go over a field to reach a gate on to a lane.

Go left along the lane to reach Moorledge where a signed path leads through the grounds of the house and across a field. Go through a gate and follow a hedge to reach a road. Turn left and follow the road into Stanton Drew village, from where a signed lane leads off to the **Stanton Drew stone circle** which lies on private land, but to which access is allowed. Now find the Druid Arms Inn, just beyond which a farm lane leads off westward, i.e. away from the stone circle. The farm lane becomes a green lane: follow it until a cottage is spotted ahead. Now go left and cross a stream over an old clapper bridge, continuing across a field heading towards a barn in the top right corner. In the next field a more obvious path leads down to the River Chew which is crossed to reach a lane. Follow this to the main B3130 which runs through the village. Do not turn left however: the main road can be dangerous, so cross it and follow the drive to **Chew Court**, going under the arch on its left side to emerge into the churchyard and the start of the walk.

POINTS OF INTEREST:

Chew Magna – Chew is a delightful place, its array of fine houses speaking of its prosperous past as a cloth-making village. The church of St Andrew is Norman and has a superb tower nearly 100 feet high. Inside there is a most unusual carved oak effigy, probably of Sir John Houteville, a 13th century knight.

Tun Bridge – The bridge is a superb example of a 15th century bridge, and has three pointed arches. Look over the eastern side (left as you follow the walk) to see a stone trough. When smallpox was ravaging the village local farmers brought food to the bridge, collecting their cash from the trough which was filled with vinegar.

Stanton Drew Stone Circle – The circle is one of the most important in the southwest. So little was (and is) known about the builders of such circles that legends grew up around them. Here the most popular is that the circle was formed from dancers petrified for having dared to dance on Sunday.

Chew Court – The Court was once the Palace of the Bishop of Bath and Wells, as well as being the local courthouse.

REFRESHMENTS:

The Pony and Trap, Knowle Hill.
The Druid Arms, Stanton Drew.
There are also several inns and cafés in Chew Magna. .

Walk 76   **COMBE ST NICHOLAS**   6m (9$\frac{1}{2}$km)

Maps: OS Sheets Landranger 193; Pathfinder ST 21/31.

A pleasant walk through hilly south Somerset.

Start: At 301113, the church at Combe St Nicholas.

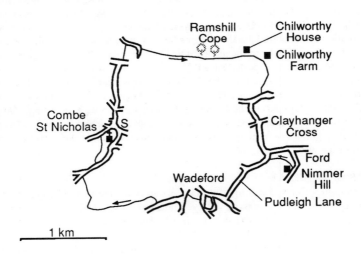

From the church head north past the Post Office and turn right, then immediately left into Church Road. Follow this to a T-junction. Go across the road into a field, follow the hedge to the left around a disused quarry and go downhill to reach a gate. Go through to a short path on to a road. Go right and walk along the road to reach two gates on the left. Go through the first gate and follow the hedge to the right. Follow the hedge through a second field, contouring around the hillside. When the hedge turns away to the right, continue on your original line, now aiming for the right side of Ranshill Copse. Go through a gate next to the Copse and walk along its edge to reach a field corner. In the next field go half-left and follow a path to reach a gate in the far left-hand corner. Go through and walk along a track past some cottages and Chilworthy House, to the left.

When the track goes left to Chilworthy Farm continue on the farm lane to reach a road. Go right to reach a road junction. Turn left and go down to another junction at Clayhanger Cross. Here, go ahead on the road signed for Pudleigh. Bear left with the road, ignoring a right turn for Wadeford. Take the next road on the right, at a bungalow, and walk down to a ford. Go over the footbridge and follow the road to reach a path on the right, signed for Pudleigh. Go up steps beside **Ninner Mill** and go left along the mill race. Go over the sluice on to a path. Cross the mill stream and walk along its bank. Go over the bridge ahead and turn left to reach a road (Pudleigh Lane).

Turn left along the lane and follow it to a T-junction. Turn right into Wadeford. Pass the Haymaker Inn and turn left into Rockstile. After about 100 yards go right on to a footpath. Go over a stile and cross a field to reach a gate on to a road. Go left to a road junction and turn right on to the Scrapton road.

After 500 yards go right through a gate on to a footpath signed for Combe St Nicholas. Cross the field and go over a stile on to a lane. Turn left and follow the lane to a gate. Go through and follow the right-hand hedge across the field to its far corner. Cross the next field to the right-hand gate opposite. Cross the field beyond to a gate. Go through and follow the left hedge up the field beyond. At the corner go right, along the field edge, and through the second gate to the left. Cross another field to a stile in the corner and go over this to a path out on to a road.

Turn right and after 200 yards turn left on to a path beside a bungalow signed for Stant Way. Go over a stile and cross a field to a gate. Cross the next field to reach an enclosed path on to a road. Turn right and walk into Combe St Nicholas, bearing right to regain the church.

POINTS OF INTEREST:

Ninner Mill – The mill was one of many in the area around Combe St Nicholas, most of them powered by water from springs that spouted from the hillside south-east of the village. This 'spring line' is caused by a change in the underlying geology, permeable rock meeting impermeable bedrock so that water which has drained down from the surface runs along the bedrock and springs out where the bedrock is exposed.

REFRESHMENTS:
The Green Dragon, Combe St Nicholas.
The Haymaker, Wadeford.

Walk 77   **BURROW MUMP**   6m (9¹/₂km)

Maps: OS Sheets Landranger 182 and 193; Pathfinder ST 22/32 and ST 23/33.

A walk in Alfred's Britain.

Start: At 360305, the National Trust car park at Burrow Mump.

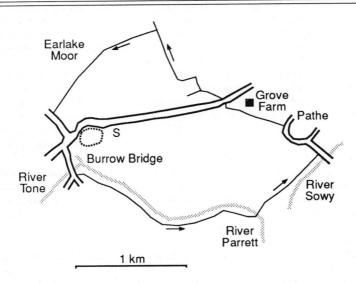

Go over the stile to **Burrow Mump** and cross it to reach a gate on to the main A361 road. Go left and cross Burrow Bridge (over the River Parrett) to reach a cross-roads. Go left on the minor road through the village of Burrow Bridge. Go over Stanmoor Bridge, where the River Tone meets the River Parrett, and go left through a gate to reach the right bank of the Tone. Go down to the rivers confluence and turn right along the Parrett's left bank. The river stays close to the road at first, but then swings away from it. Follow it, but where it turns sharply right, back towards the road, go over a footbridge.

Go left beyond the bridge, going through a gate and crossing a field to reach another gate. Go through and bear right towards the bank of another, smaller river (the River Sowy). Now follow the bank to reach a road. Turn left and walk to a

T-junction. Turn left and follow the road through the hamlet of Pathe. The road bears right, out of the village, reaching the converted Pathe Barn to the left. Go up the drive on its far side to reach a gate. Go through a field to reach another gate. Go through and follow the right hedge across two fields to reach Grove Farm. Go through the gate ahead – always maintaining the same direction – and cross to reach a gate on to a track. Go right for a short distance to reach the main A361.

The short way back to the start is to turn left here, following the roadside for $^3/_4$ mile (1,200 metres). For those who do not wish to take this busy short cut, cross the road to reach a bridlepath. Follow this for 200 yards to a junction. Go right. In the next 400 yards the bridlepath goes sharp left, then sharp right. Walk another 200 yards to another junction. Do not turn left: instead, go ahead for another 350 yards to reach another junction. Go left here, following the bridlepath to a road. Turn left and walk down to the road's junction with the A361. Now reverse the outward route back to the start.

POINTS OF INTEREST:

Burrow Mump – In 1963 a piece of jewellery was discovered near Athelney – about 2 miles south of our route. It is probable that the piece once formed the top of a staff. It consists of an enamelled figure behind a plate of rock crystal, the whole surrounded by worked gold. It bears the inscription AELFRED MEL HEHT GEWYRCAN – Alfred had me made. The piece is one of the finest Anglo-Saxon works of art to have been discovered to date, and is a beautiful link to an interesting period in English history. In 878 King Alfred had fled to Somerset to escape the Danish invaders of England. There he discovered the Isle of Athelney, an area of land raised above the protective marshes of the Somerset Levels. Close by was Burrow Mump, a natural look-out. Alfred rested and recovered. If there is any truth at all in the legend then it was here he burnt the cakes. And it was from here that he set out to meet, and resoundingly defeat, the Danes at the battle of Ethandun on the southern side of the Polden Hills.

REFRESHMENTS:
The King Alfred Inn, Burrow Bridge.

Walk 78   **CROSCOMBE**   6m (9¹/₂km)

Maps: OS Sheets Landranger 183; Pathfinder ST 44/54 and
ST 64/74.

A fine country walk that visits an old fort.

Start: At 591444, Croscombe church.

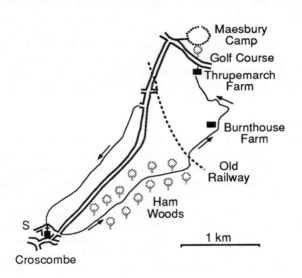

From the western end of the church go up Church Lane. Go right up Rock Street to
the junction with Thrupe Lane. Cross and take the lane opposite to reach a gate beyond
a house. Go through and follow a fence into a shallow valley. Bear left along the
valley to reach a stile beside a gate. Go over, or through, to reach Ham Woods. Follow
the main path through the wood, ignoring all side turnings. The path bears gently
right, then equally gently back left towards a now visible, to the left, railway viaduct.
Leave the path here, going up to the left hand end of the viaduct to find a gate.

Cross the old railway track – this was once the Somerset and Dorset railway (*see*
Note to Walk 18/19) – and go through the gate on the other side. Cross the field
ahead, aiming for the right-hand of two gates. Go through and follow the left edge to
another gate. Go through and bear left to reach a farm track turning along it to reach

Burnthouse Farm. Go through the farmyard and go left by the tanks into a field. Go through a gate into a field in which there is a fine row of oaks. Walk to the end of the oaks to reach a green lane. Follow the lane into a field and go diagonally across to reach a gate. Walk to Thrupemarsh Farm, going between the farmhouse and the farm buildings to reach a metalled lane. Follow this to a road.

Go left along the road, passing a golf course and wood to the right to reach a signed path over a stile, also to the right. If you reach a road to the left, you have walked 50 yards too far. Go over the stile and bear right towards the top corner of a wood. Go through a gate on to **Maesbury Camp**.

Reverse the route to the road, go right and after 50 yards go left on the road to Dinder and Croscombe. Follow the road under the old railway to reach a junction. Bear left on the Croscombe road. About 200 yards from the junction you will reach a green lane to the right. Follow the lane, keeping along it when it becomes metalled. The lane drops down into **Croscombe** leaving you with a short walk through the village to regain the church.

POINTS OF INTEREST:

Maesbury Camp – The Camp is an Iron Age hillfort, and it is easy to see why it was positioned here. Not only does the natural, oval, hill offer added defences to the man-made ditches and ramparts, but the view is outstanding in all directions. Those seeking protection from an enemy would have had an unrivalled view of movements in the valleys below. When the Romans came they built their road from the Mendip lead mines to the south coast so that it passed close to the camp, so it is likely that its defensive qualities were not lost on those most impressive of soldiers.

Croscombe – Croscombe is an elegant little village, but is most noteworthy for its church. When this area of Somerset became prosperous as a result of the wool industry many of the local squire families exhibited their wealth by building great houses, and equally grand monuments to themselves in the village church. The Croscombe Fortescues were different, choosing to use their cash to furnish the church, as a result of which it has the most impressive Jacobean furnishings in Somerset. Best of all are the box pews, the roofed pulpit and the rood screen.

Finally in the village, have a look at the 14th century cross. In the 19th century the lord of the manor decided to have it demolished, but it was successfully defended by the village folk, armed with sticks.

REFRESHMENTS:

The Bull Terrier, Long Street, Croscombe.
The George, Croscombe.

Walk 79   **NEWTON PARK AND STANTON PRIOR**   6m (9½km)
Maps: OS Sheets Landranger 172; Pathfinder ST 66/76.
A walk near two of Avon's archaeological features.
Start: At 701649, the church in Newton St Loe.

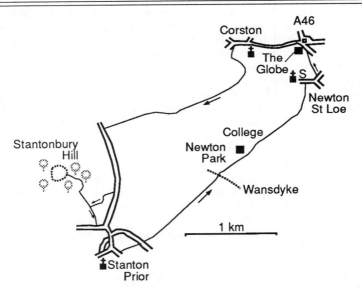

From the church take the road back into **Newton St Loe**, but soon go left on a signed
path that crosses a field to reach The Globe, a famous inn on a roundabout of the A4
Bath-Bristol road. Follow the road edge from the inn into the village of Carston. Pass
the church and turn left down a lane. Pass Manor Farm, staying with the lane as it
climbs towards woodland. Stay with the lane as it swings to the right through the
wood. Where it ends continue ahead on a path across fields, aiming at Stantonbury
Hill ahead. Soon a ruin – the inappropriately named New Barn – is reached. Stay with
the path beyond the ruin: it bears left over a stream, then follows the left side of a field
to reach a road. Turn left towards Stanton Prior.

   After about 800 yards a stile on the right gives access to a path. Follow this
along, then through, a hedge. Take the left hedge in the next field, then go along its far
hedge to reach a wood. Go up through this to the top of **Stantonbury Hill**. From the

hill top the route can be reversed, or the waymarked path can be followed downhill, going through several gates to arrive on a road. Turn left to a staggered cross-roads. There turn right, but not sharply back right, to reach **Stanton Prior**. In the village, go right into a narrow No Through Road to reach the church.

To continue, with the church at your back go right past a small chapel to reach a cross-roads. Bear right, then cross to reach a stile. Go over and follow the waymarked path to a road. Cross this to reach a stile and follow the right side of the next two fields to reach a footbridge and a stile into a green lane. Turn right and follow the lane to its end. There go over a stile and follow a path uphill. The path crosses the line of the **Wansdyke**, which is not easy to discern, though it is more easily seen a little way to the right. Continue towards the buildings of Newton Park College ahead, crossing a stile on to the college playing fields, then the playing fields themselves.

A metalled drive is now reached: follow this through the college grounds and back to a road in Newton St Loe. Cross and take the lane opposite back to the church.

POINTS OF INTEREST:

Newton St Loe – The village's name derives from its first Norman lord, Geoffrey, Bishop of Loe. The debate about whether St Loe is from the French *cinq l'eau*, five springs, goes on. There are several fine buildings in the village, one in unusual William-and-Mary style, another a Free School, founded in 1698 by Richard Jones. Not for two more centuries was the idea of general education to take firm root.

Stantonsbury Hill – The Hill is topped by an Iron Age hillfort, and also formed part of the Wansdyke.

Stanton Prior – The second part of the name derives from the time when Bath Priory owned the village. The church of St Lawrence dates from that time, though there was a great deal of restoration in the 19th century. There is a village legend that the yew tree in the churchyard was planted on a plague pit, that is a large hole into which victims of the Black Death were tipped.

Wansdyke – Little is known about this earthwork. It is thought to have run from the Bristol Channel to the Marlborough Downs, but as it is difficult to follow for all of its route that is not definite. Why was it built? There is no definite answer to that question. The probable age of the earthwork is late Celtic, say the 4th or 5th centuries. That is also assumed to have been when the battle of Badon was fought between King Arthur's Celts and the Saxons, so some have suggested the Wansdyke was part of the Celtic defences against the invading Saxons.

REFRESHMENTS:
The Globe Inn, near Newton St Loe.

Walk 80   **WIVELISCOMBE**   6m (9¹/₂km)

Maps: OS Sheets Landranger 181; Pathfinder ST 02/12.

A walk from the old town of Wiveliscombe.

Start: At 081278, the North Street car park, Wiveliscombe.

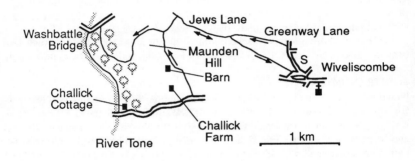

From the car park go back to North Street and turn right. Go past the Fire Station, to the right, and the school, to the left, then cross the road to turn left into Greenway Lane. Follow the lane uphill to a Y-junction, bearing right there into Jews Lane and following it to the top of the hill ahead. Just beyond the hilltop the lane reaches a Y-junction. Go sharply left here on the lane signed for Challick. Walk along the lane for ³/₄ mile (1,200 metres) to where it ends at a gate. Go through and continue for 80 yards to reach a gate on the right. Go through this and walk along the wood edge for 100 yards before going half-right to reach a path to a gate. Go through the gate into the wood. Follow the path down through the wood, going over at a crossing of tracks. The path exits the wood on to a road. Go left to reach Washbattle Bridge over the River Tone.

Do not go over the bridge: instead go left along a track, then bear right to a path along the left bank of the Tone. The path follows the river all the way to the road at

Challick Cottage. Go left, uphill, on the road, passing Challick Farm on the left. About 200 yards further on a track signed for Maundown Top is reached on the left. Take this to reach a cluster of five gates. Go through the second gate from the left and follow the left hedge across the field beyond to reach a gate. Go through and turn right, going between a barn, to the left, and the field hedge. Follow the path ahead, which goes across **Maundown Hill**, the summit of which is off to the left.

The path reaches the outward route at a lane end. From here the outward route can be followed, but for a better look at **Wiveliscombe** it is better to bear right at the Y-junction at the end of Jews Lane, walking down the road to reach the Town Square. From there the town's church is to the right, while the car park start point is to the left.

POINTS OF INTEREST:

Maundown Hill – Though this is essentially a low-level route, Maundown Hill reaching only 1,007 feet (307 metres) above sea level, it does offer a surprisingly good view of the early valley of the River Tone, usually called Taunton Deane.

Wiveliscombe – This attractive little market town has an equally attractive name, one that has been known to give visitors to Somerset a real tongue-twisting problem. The name is pronounced *Wivel-is-cum*, but is usually shortened to *Wivvy* by the locals. Though there is local evidence of Iron Age and Roman settlements, virtually everything in the town today dates from its previous period as market town to Taunton Deane, that is, from the late 18th and early 19th centuries. Of the buildings, one of the most interesting is actually a little later, the Court House, built in 1881 with carved wooden wall tiling. It now houses the town library and is passed by the suggested return route to the Town Square.

The town church dates from the prosperous era, an earlier one having been rebuilt in 1829. The church, a fine red sandstone building, has a large array of catacombs beneath it, and these were used to store many of Britain's most valuable art treasures during the 1939–45 War. A plaque in the church lists the treasures: most of them are household names.

POINTS OF INTEREST:

The Bear Inn, North Street, Wiveliscombe.
The White Hart Hotel, West Street, Wiveliscombe.

Maps: OS Sheets Landranger 172; Pathfinder ST 49/59 and
ST 69/79.

A walk along the banks of the River Severn.

Start: At 609924, near the Anchor Inn, Oldbury-on-Severn.

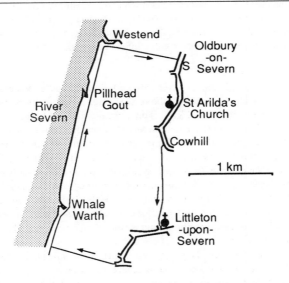

From the Anchor Inn take the village road southward. The road climbs, but only
gently, and passes the village school to reach **St Arilda's Church**. Continue along the
road to the hamlet of Cowhill, ignoring a No Through Road to the right in favour of
staying on the 'main' road through the village. Soon you will reach a cottage, on the
right, which is set side on to the road. The cottage's gate has a painted sign for Littleton:
go through – it really is a right of way! – and cross the garden to reach an orchard. Go
through the orchard, bearing left to reach a stile. Go over, and cross the field ahead,
following the left hedge. In the next field stay with the hedge, heading eventually for
a small wooded hill. Go to the left of the wood to reach a path that heads for the now
visible village of **Littleton-upon-Severn**.

The path emerges on to a road close to Littleton church. Turn right towards the village centre. Take the next turning left, signed for Eberton, to pass the White Hart Inn and the Post Office. Beyond is the Evangelical Church: turn right opposite it on a lane that deteriorates the closer it gets to the River Severn. By the time **Littleton Warth** and the river embankment is reached the track is merely a path. Turn right, walking past the inlets of **Whale Warth** and the elegantly named Pillhead Gout to reach Westland, a more substantial inlet where a local sailing club has its moorings. Here the embankment turns inland, then peters out, the path following the southern bank of the inlet towards the village of **Oldbury-on-Severn**. This path leads directly back to the Anchor Inn, the start of the walk.

POINTS OF INTEREST:

St Arilda's church – The church stands on Cow Hill, for which the nearby hamlet is named. Arilda was a local Saxon girl who was beheaded by the lord of the manor for being virtuous enough to choose death rather than consent to adultery. She is buried in Gloucester Cathedral. In the 18th century the church was white washed so that it could better act as a landmark to sailors on the Severn.

Littleton-upon-Severn – Like Oldbury, Littleton is 'on-Severn' despite being some way from the river. The reason was the capricious nature of the Severn, which frequently flooded the land on its margins. The tidal rise of the river is one of the highest in the world, and the tidal race – known as the Severn Bore – is famous. Until the building of the embankment flooding of the bankside fields was frequent.

Littleton Warth – A warth is an old local name for an inlet of the sea, other names being pill and gout. Today the name is more often applied to this section of the river bank. Hereabouts the remains of putchers, the conical wicker baskets used by Severn fishermen to catch salmon, can occasionally be seen. Also to be seen are flocks of water birds, the Severn estuary being a famous transit area for migrants, and a winter feeding area for ducks, geese, swans and waders.

Whale Warth – This inlet was so named after a whale was stranded there in 1885.

Oldbury-on-Severn – The inn names, Ship and Anchor, give a clue to the village's past as a Severn port. Distinctly more modern is the nuclear power station which shares the village name. The blue and white cylinders house reactors of Britain's first generation type, known as Magnox.

REFRESHMENTS:

The Anchor, Oldbury-on-Severn.
The Ship, Oldbury-on-Severn.
The White Hart, Littleton-upon-Severn.

Walk 82   **HINTON CHARTERHOUSE**   6¹/₂m (10¹/₂km)

Maps: OS Sheets Landranger 172; Pathfinder ST 65/75 and ST 66/96.

A picturesque walk which passes a ruined priory.

Start: At 772582, the centre of Hinton Charterhouse.

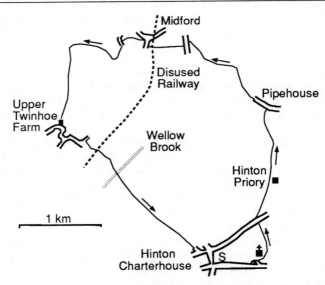

From the main street in Hinton Charterhouse – the B3110 road – go south, then left at the cross-roads on to a road that leads to the village church of St John the Baptist. Go into the churchyard and follow the path as it bears right before reaching the far corner. Go left along the churchyard wall and through a swing gate at the churchyard end. Go over a stile into a large field. Take the path which heads for the conifers peeping over the rise ahead passing, to the left, the 18th century Hinton House.

Go to the left of the conifers and walk towards a row of trees. Go over a stile in the row to reach a road. Cross the road and the stile beyond, going half-right in the field beyond. The ruins of **Hinton Priory** can now be seen to the right. Cross a stile next to a tall ash tree and follow the direction of a waymarker to reach a hunting gate. Go through and follow the hedge on the right to a stile. Go over and cross to a stile.

Go across the next field to the top left corner where there is a stile. Go over this and two further fields to reach a farm track, with a chicken farm to the right. Go through a paddock and a garden to reach a lane. Go left through the hamlet of Pipehouse.

Beyond a thatched cottage the lane becomes a rough track. After 1 mile it reaches the B3110 road. Cross the road and go left to pass some buildings. At their end go right to a footbridge over Wellow Brook. Cross a field towards a disused railway viaduct. Go over a stile and under the viaduct. Go right to reach the B3110 again. Turn right and right again on to a footpath opposite the Hope and Anchor Inn. This footpath goes under the viaduct again and then under the route you have just walked in order to reach a stile on to the bed of a **drained canal**. The path continues along what was the towpath of the canal. The path soon reaches the embankment of an old railway. Go over a stile and under the embankment. Cross a stile and a field to regain the old towpath: follow it along the valley of the Cam Brook until a footbridge on the left allows the Cam to be crossed.

The path climbs uphill to reach a track to Upper Twinhoe Farm. Where it reaches a road go left, and go left again at a road junction. Pass Leesons Cottage and turn right towards Middle Twinhoe Farm. Go left before the house to reach a gate and stile by a barn. Go over and keep to the hedge on the left to reach a stile. Go half-left to reach a gap in the field corner. Beyond is a grass lane: follow it downhill past Lower Twinhoe Farm. At a T-junction go right and downhill, going under the railway bridge and down to Wellow Brook. Go over a footbridge and continue along a path, soon using a plank bridge to the left to reach a wood. Go right along the wood edge for 150 yards to reach another plank bridge. Cross and follow the path to a gate.

Cross a field to reach a narrow valley. Walk down this going through several gates to reach a track that reaches some houses. Beyond, a metalled lane climbs into Hinton Charterhouse. Go left to reach the B3110 and the start of the walk.

POINTS OF INTEREST:

Hinton Priory – The Carthusian Order of monks was founded in 1184 by St Bruno at Grand Charterhouse in Provence. The Carthusian Priories, or Charterhouses, consisted of single cells occupied by the monks, together with a church. Hinton was one of Britain's earliest charterhouses, having been founded in 1232. The Charterhouse gave the extra name to the village of Hinton.

Drained Canal – Once carried coal from Radstock to the Kennet and Avon Canal.

REFRESHMENTS:

The Hope and Anchor, Midford.
The Stag, Hinton Charterhouse.

Walk 83   **FYNE COURT**   6¹/₂m (10¹/₂km)

Maps: OS Sheets Landranger 182; Pathfinder ST 23/33.
A walk on the southern tail of the Quantocks.
Start: At 222321, the car park at Fyne Court.

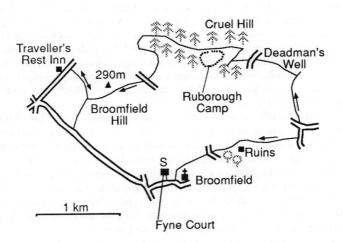

The Court is not easy to find, but is close to the hamlet of Broomfield which lies about 5 miles (8km) to the west of North Petherton. By contrast, the walk is easy to follow, having been waymarked by the Somerset Trust for Nature Conservation – who have their headquarters in Fyne Court. The waymarker is the figure 5, in yellow, inside a circle of arrows.

From **Fyne Court** go back to the road and turn left into **Broomfield**. The church is worth visiting, but the route does not reach it, going left just before on a downhill path. The path reaches a road: cross to a stile into a wood. The path beyond climbs through the wood emerging into open country near some old buildings. Go to the left of these and stay with the path to reach a road. Turn left past two houses to reach a T-junction. Go left, then almost immediately turn right and cross the road to reach a signed bridlepath, following it as it becomes a narrower path. The path goes downhill

156

to a waymarker that points the way leftward along a fence to **Deadman's Well**. From the Well the path rises to reach a road. Cross to reach the Forestry Commission's Wind Down plantation. At the first track junction go right and climb **Cruel Hill**, passing **Ruborough Camp**. After about 800 yards, where the track turns right, go left on a bridlepath that continues upwards to emerge on to open farmland. Follow the right-hand hedge across this, going past a small reservoir to reach a road.

Cross and follow the path opposite across Broomfield Hill, bearing right at each of two Y-junctions. Beyond the second, as a beech tree-lined path is reached, a stile on the right gives access to a path that can be followed to the Traveller's Rest Inn, a detour of about $3/_4$ mile (1,200 metres) out and back. Follow the tree-lined path to a road. Turn left and walk to a road junction. Bear right here, and then turn first left towards Broomfield. Fyne Court and the start of the walk is about 250 yards along, on the left-hand side.

POINTS OF INTEREST:

Fyne Court – The original Court was built in the early 17th century, but was largely destroyed by fire in 1898. The remnants are now owned by the National Trust and form the headquarters of the Somerset Trust for Nature Conservancy. The Court was built for the Crosse family whose most famous son was Andrew, an early 19th century gentleman scientist who performed obscure experiments with the latest discovery – electricity – and whose associates claimed had once created life, an insect, by passing a current through an unidentified liquid. The Court is open all year, daily from 9am – 6pm or sunset if earlier.

Broomfield – What is now little more than a hamlet was once a sizeable village, depopulated when folk moved off the land late last century. The church has a good brass, dated at 1443, of Richard Dulverton, the rector, though the head is sadly missing.

Deadman's Well – A Domesday settlement now long gone, though the remains of houses can still be seen.

Cruel Hill – So called because it was vicious work for horses pulling carts up its length.

Ruborough Camp – Experts believe that the camp, which probably had an Iron Age origin, was occupied by the Romans at a later time.

REFRESHMENTS:

Fyne Court offers teas on Sundays and Bank Holidays in summer, and has picnic sites. Otherwise the detour to the Traveller's Rest Inn must be followed.

Walk 84   **MARSHFIELD** $6^1/_2$m ($10^1/_2$km)

Maps: OS Sheets Landranger 172; Pathfinder ST 67/77.

A high wold walk, using part of the Cotswold Way.

Start: At 751728, Cold Ashton church.

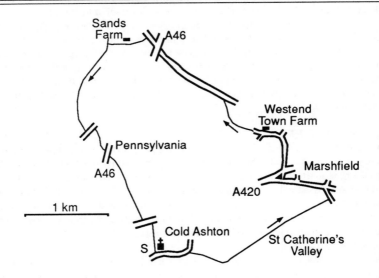

From **Cold Ashton Church** the Cotswold Way goes right, passing **Cold Ashton Manor** to reach the main A46. Our walk goes left, passing the last houses of the village to reach, to the right, a footpath signed for Marshfield. Follow this, going downhill to a gate, and continuing downhill on the rough track beyond. The track bears left around the hillside to reach a stream that flows into St Catherine's Brook. Follow the path to a ruin, beyond which are the upper reaches of St Catherine's Valley. The path crosses a long field, going through a gap to reach another. In the next field, reached by gate or stile, the path joins the brook, following it to its source on the hillside. Beyond the source, continue in the same direction until a fence is reached. Go right and up towards trees to reach a pair of stiles. Go over and left along the green lane until it goes left. There cross the stile ahead and follow a path through two fields to St Martin's Lane. Go left to reach **Marshfield**.

Walk along High Street, turning right opposite Green Lane to reach the main A420. Cross and take the lane opposite to Westend Town Farm. Pass the farm to reach a Y-junction. Take the right arm and soon after go over a double stile in the wall on the right. Follow a wall and track downhill, but where these bear left walk ahead to a footbridge. Beyond head for the central electricity pole, going over a stile and a field to reach a gate. Do not go through: instead, turn right into a green lane. Go through a gate and uphill to a lane. Go left and follow the lane to the A46. Cross and go right, then left almost immediately on to the road for Dyrham. After 100 yards a gate on the left is reached – unsigned, but across from another gate. Go through and follow the wall and hedge on the right downhill. Go through a gate and follow a path towards Sands Farm. Just before the farm turn right through a gate to reach, shortly, the farm lane. Go left along it, but right off of it before the farmhouse is reached. Go past several ponds and turn left along the hedge ahead. You have now reached the Cotswold Way, the rest of the route following its excellent waymarkers.

The Way heads south, then goes uphill and through woodland, firstly a narrow copse, then a more substantial wood. Beyond, stay close to the wall on the left to reach a road. Go left along the verge for 100 yards or so, then cross to reach a waymarker. Follow the hedge to reach a track to Pensylvania and the main A46. Cross the road to reach a stile. Go diagonally up the field beyond to reach a stile. Go half-left to a stile on to the A420. Go left to reach the White Hart Inn. Now cross the road to reach a gate into the churchyard of Cold Ashton church, the start of the walk.

POINTS OF INTEREST:

Cold Ashton Church – The village church was rebuilt at the expense of Thomas Key, the rector in the early 16th century. In several places the rector's motif of a T and a key entwined can be seen.

Cold Ashton Manor – The manor is Elizabethan and has been called the most perfect example of its type in England.

Marshfield – The curious name of the village, whose position on the exposed high wold makes it an unlikely spot for a marsh, derives from *march*, or boundary. Close to where our route leaves the village are a row of early 17th century almshouses built to house eight old folk of the village.

REFRESHMENTS:

The White Hart Inn, Cold Ashton.
The Swan Inn, Pennsylvania.
The Crown Inn, High Street, Marshfield.
The Catherine Wheel, High Street, Marshfield.

Walk 85   **CREWKERNE**   7m (11km)

Maps: OS Sheets Landranger 193; Pathfinder ST 40/50.
A quiet, pleasant walk through rural country.
Start: The West Street car park, Crewkerne.

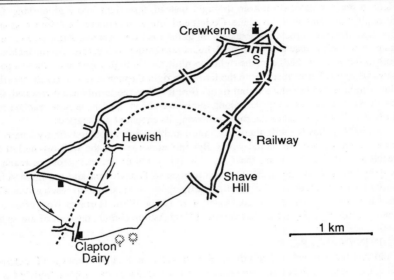

The car park is signed (for the Bowling Club) from the main A30 road.

Go out of the car park and turn left along the main road for 100 yards. Go left into Lyewater and follow it to reach an enclosed footpath on the right. Go through a gate and cross to another. Go through on to a path that leads to a road. Go left and follow the road to a cross-roads. Go straight over and walk down to Hewish. Turn left there and go under the railway. Cross a stream and turn right into a No Through Road. Walk along the road to reach a footbridge. Do not cross: instead go left through a gate into a field. Go diagonally across the field, aiming at the houses, to reach a stile. Go over and turn right along a road. Go over a footbridge and a crossing lane and walk past Lyminster Farm, to the left, to reach a road junction.

About 20 yards further there is a gate on the left: go through and follow the right-hand hedge across a field. Stay with the right-hand hedge across the next field, but where it swings right leave it and bear left towards a tree in the centre of the field, continuing beyond the tree to reach a gate in the right-hand field corner. Go through and then right along a stream to reach a footbridge. Cross and turn left to walk back along the stream to a kissing gate. Go through on to a road and go left, under the railway bridge, to reach a T-junction with the B3165. Turn right along the road edge to reach Clapton Dairy, to the left, and turn into it. Walk through the yard to reach a gate on to a bridleway. Walk uphill, going through several gates to reach a small wood on the right. The bridleway follows the wood edge, but when this turns right, it goes left, crossing fields to reach a road near a house. Turn right for 200 yards to a cross-roads. Turn left and walk steeply down Shave Hill towards Crewkerne. Go over the railway and continue to a T-junction. Turn left to reach another T-junction. Turn right along the B3165 and walk down into **Crewkerne**. Go past a school and turn left into West Street to return to the car park.

POINTS OF INTEREST:

Crewkerne – The town has a long and illustrious history having been home to a mint in Saxon times, a fact that made it very prosperous. In medieval times it was less prosperous, but as a cloth-making town it achieved better times, becoming famous for its sailcloth, winning a contract to supply the Royal Navy and claiming to have made the sails for Nelson's *Victory*. Ironically, Capt Hardy who held the dying Nelson was educated in Crewkerne, at the Grammar School – now Church Hall – in Abbey Street. The town also made the sails for several challengers for the Americas Cup, but as these all lost it is much less of a claim to fame. Later, the cloth-making skills of the townsfolk were put to use in making parachute harnesses during the 1939–45 War.

A further claim to fame is that a local man ran one of Britain's earliest postal services, utilising the Plymouth to London coach service that over-nighted in the town.

The town church, to St Bartholomew, has a very fine west front.

REFRESHMENTS:

None on route, though the Blue Bay Inn, Clapton, is only 150 yards or so south of Clapton Dairy. There are numerous possibilities in Crewkerne.

KILCOTT MILL 7m (11km)

Maps: OS Sheets Landranger 172; Pathfinder ST 68/78.
A fine walk which includes a section of the Cotswold Way.
Start: At 769896, the car park in the village of Hillesley.

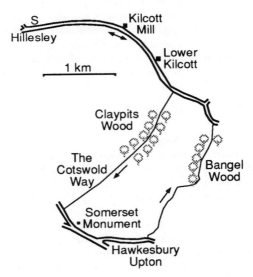

From the village take the lane to Kilcott, a charming lane, narrow and hedged and, in later stages, with a stream on its border. However, the narrowness does mean that the walker needs to be cautious of cars. Go past **Kilcott Mill** and its mill pond, and continue past a farm on the left side, an early house in the small hamlet of Lower Kilcott. Now look for a signed footpath on the right-hand side of the lane. It is marked for Hawkesbury and its monument, and also has a Cotswold Way sticker. Note that this is the *second* sign for Hawkesbury, but the only one with a Cotswold waymarker.

The Cotswold Way follows a distinct track to, and into, the woodland of Claypit and Frith woods. Within the wood the Way is occasionally a little less distinct, but is always obvious. When the Way emerges from the woods, head for a barn on the skyline. The barn is on the opposite side of a road on to which the path emerges. Open ground is passed on this section of the walk, and the slender Hawkesbury, or Somerset, Monument can be seen to the left.

Turn left on the road and follow it to the **Monument**. Continue down the road to reach the first houses of Hawkesbury Upton, taking the turning to the left, signed for 'Starveall', as they are reached. Follow this new lane for about 400 yards to reach a short track on the left which leads to a gate. Go through and follow the clear path heading north-east to reach a gate into a field. Cross a field to another gate, and cross the field beyond to yet another gate. Beyond this gate the path descends the hillside, reaching a stream that carves a delicate valley through Bangel and Stickstey Woods. Follow the stream down to a lane. Turn left on this lane to reach the outward journey at Lower Kilcott. Now retrace your steps to Hillesley.

POINTS OF INTEREST:

Kilcott Mill – The name Kilcott is of disputed origin. Some experts see a Celtic origin, from *Kil-y-coed*, the wooded valley, while others incline to a later, Saxon, name, from *Cylla Cot*, Cylla's cottage.

The Kilcott stream fell sharply from the Cotswold edge and was used to power several mills. A mill on one side of the present Kilcott Mill was mentioned in the Domesday Book, though the buildings the walker sees were erected in 1655. Most of the mills on the stream were for fulling, part of the process of making wool, the woollen industry having made the Cotswolds the rich area it was in the 16th and later centuries. Kilcott was also a fulling mill, though it had once been a corn mill, the stream driving an 18 foot waterwheel. The mill pond is proverbially calm.

Hawkesbury Monument – The monument was raised in 1846 to the memory of General Lord Robert Edward Henry Somerset, the General's family name explaining the alternative name of Somerset Monument. The General was a member of the Beaufort family from nearby Badminton and served under Wellington at the Battle of Waterloo. For a small fee the walker can climb the 144 steps to the top of the tower. From there the view is expansive, covering virtually all of the route.

REFRESHMENTS:

The Duke of Beaufort Inn, Hawkesbury Upton.

Walk 87   **THE KENNET AND AVON CANAL**   7m (11km)

Maps: OS Sheets Landranger 172; Pathfinder ST 66/76.

A delightful walk, half of which is on the canal towpath.

Start: At 783626, the lay-by on the A36 near Dundas Aqueduct.

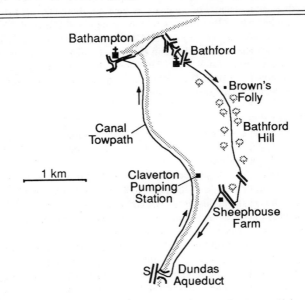

From the lay-by follow the signed path down to the **Dundas Aqueduct**. From the wharf beside it go across the footbridge over the canal and turn left along the towpath, following what is now part of the Avon Walkway all the way to Bathampton, a journey of about 3 miles (5 km), passing on the way the **Claverton Pumping Station**. Close to Bathampton bridge a lane (Tyning Road) runs parallel to the towpath: use this to reach **Bathampton church**.

From the church go back along Tyning Road following it to a level crossing. Cross the railway and go half-left on a footpath which heads for a railway bridge and electricity transmission tower (pylon). Go over the bridge to reach the main A363 road. Cross and turn right. Go under the transmission lines and turn left into Bathford. Go right into Oslings Lane almost immediately, bearing left with it to reach St Swithin's, Bathford's church. Take the footpath to the left of the church to reach

Pump Lane. Go right, then left into Mountain Wood, going right shortly after to reach a stile on to open ground. Go diagonally uphill across this to reach a stile at the start of the Brown's Folly Nature Reserve. Follow the path up through the woodland of the Reserve. Note that this path does not go to **Brown's Folly**.

Follow the path, which stays close to a stone wall that is the border between Avon and Wiltshire along the top of Bathford Hill, and then descend the hill to reach the main A363. Turn left for 50 yards to reach the Wiltshire border sign. Now cross and go through a gate. Follow the path beyond from which there are fine valley views and from which Claverton's American Museum can also be seen. The path soon descends to reach a road. Go right, following the road downhill to Sheephouse Farm. Go through the farmyard and follow the path ahead downhill to reach the River Avon. Go left along the river bank to reach Dundas Aqueduct. There, go up steps to the Aqueduct and cross it to reach the wharf. From there retrace your steps to the start.

POINTS OF INTEREST:

Dundas Aqueduct – The aqueduct carries the Kennet and Avon canal over the river Avon and the railway, a total of 150 yards. The central arch, a semi-circle is in fine style, and very picturesque, its qualities added to by the rich warmth of the local Bath stone. The aqueduct's curious name is explained by an inscription on the southern side – is named for Charles Dundas, chairman of the Canal Company at the time of its construction.

Claverton Pumping Station – The station pumped water from the River Avon to the canal using a waterwheel and a pair of beam engines. The station was built in 1813. It has now been restored, together with its 24-foot waterwheel and is open to the public from April to October on Sundays 10am – 5pm.

Bathampton church – The Viscount du Barry, a nephew of Louis XV of France's most famous mistress, is buried in the church. He was the victim of the last legal duel fought in England, dying at the hand of his friend, Col Rice, after a quarrel.

Brown's Folly – The folly is a stone tower built in 1849 by a local quarry owner called Wade Brown.

REFRESHMENTS:
The George, Bathampton.
The Crown, Bathford.
The Viaduct Inn lies about 100 yards south of the Dundas Aqueduct.

Walk 88   BICKNOLLER AND HALSWAY MANOR   7m (11km)

Maps: OS Sheets Landranger 181; Pathfinder ST 04/14.

A fine walk, combining open hill and an historic building.

Start: At 111394, Bicknoller church.

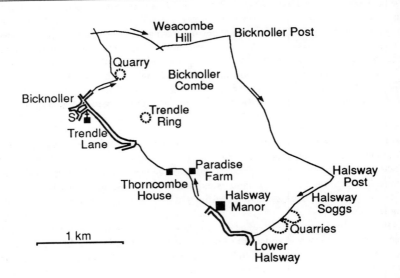

From the church go north to reach a T-junction. Go left, soon bearing right past the triangle. Now go first right up Hill Lane, heading uphill towards the Quantock ridge. Where the metalled road ends there is a gate. Go through and follow the path beyond to a junction of paths close to an old quarry. Go left here on the bridlepath signed for Weacombe. After 800 yards a path junction is reached. Go right here, following the sign for Bicknoller Post. The route goes up a bare combe, then reaches the open ridge of Weacombe Hill. Bear left on the wider track at a junction to reach the Great Road – as the Quantock ridge track is called – at Bicknoller Post, an old boundary marker.

Turn right along the Great Road to reach, after 500 yards, a second boundary post at the head of Bicknoller Combe. A right turn here offers a short-cut to the quarry passed on the outward route. Continue along the Great Road for a further mile (1,600 metres) to reach Halsway Post. Turn right here and head down Halsway Combe, staying to the right initially to avoid the marshland of the aptly-named Halsway Soggs. At a path junction cross the stream and continue on the downhill path, passing old quarries to the left.

The path reaches a road. Go right through Lower Halsway, staying with the road as it passes **Halsway Manor**. Just beyond the manor the road goes sharply left. Continue on the No Through Road, bearing right once, to reach Paradise Farm, to the right. Do not go up to the farm: instead continue along the lane to pass Thorncombe House. Stay with the lane to its junction with a road. Go right here, along **Trendle Lane**, back into **Bicknoller**. At the junction reached on the outward journey go left back to the church.

POINTS OF INTEREST:

Halsway Manor – The Manor's name is pronounced *Haulsey* by the locals, despite its spelling. The earliest reference to a house on the site was in the Domesday book when Alric, a Saxon held it. Since then it has been rebuilt, extended and restored, so that it now appears in a collection of styles, admirably suited to its present role as a residential Arts Centre.

Trendle Lane – The lane takes it name from the nearby Trendle Ring, a circular earthwork that, it is believed, was the site of a cattle pen or, perhaps, a small village. The Ring is probably Neolithic (New Stone) or Bronze Age.

Bicknoller – This pleasant little village was often the target for Quantock walks by Samuel Taylor Coleridge and William and Dorothy Wordsworth when the former lived at Nether Stowey, and the latter pair at Alfoxton. Like many of today's walkers they found refreshment at the village inn. The village church is a fine Perpendicular building with a beautiful rood screen and superbly carved bench ends. The stained glass is 20th century, by Christopher Webb.

REFRESHMENTS:
The Bicknoller Inn, Church Lane, Bicknoller.

Maps: OS Sheets Landranger 172; Pathfinder ST 66/76.
A good walk for views, following part of the Cotswold Way.
Start: At 699669, Kelston Church.

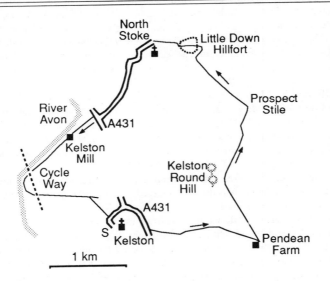

From the church walk to the main village road in Kelston, turn right and walk to the main A431 Bristol to Bath road. Turn right and follow the road towards Bath. Just beyond the last buildings there is a gate on the left. Go through and bear right on a track that contours around – though gently climbing – the southern flank of Kelston Round Hill. When the track ends continue on a path that keeps to the right of patches of woodland on the hillside. Cross several fields to reach a lane near farm buildings. Go right with the lane to Pendeen Farm, turning left shortly on to the Cotswold Way.

The well waymarked Way climbs to the right of the tree-covered Kelston Round Hill. Sadly the hill itself is not on the Way, or on a right of way despite the stile, and so technically can only be admired from a (short) distance. However, most walkers do cross the stile and visit the hill top from where there are spectacular views of the Avon Valley and the Mendips, and of the Cotswold Edge along Lansdown.

The Cotswold Way skirts the Hill, crosses a track and continues to Prospect Stile, named for the spectacular view it offers. The fact that Kelston Round Hill fills the foreground only adds to the view. Go over the stile and turn left along the Cotswold edge, the Way finding room between the edge and Bath racecourse. When the bank and ditch which defines the **Little Down Hillfort** appear, go right with it until a sign points out the Way across the hillfort.

At the far side the Cotswold Way goes right, but we take the path which descends straightforwardly towards **North Stoke**. When a track is reached, go right to reach the church, then go left through the village. Follow the road as it descends, the last few hundred yards being steeply downhill, to reach the A431. Turn right along the main road but shortly cross to reach a stile on the far side. Go over and cross a field beside the River Avon. Cross a stream to reach **Kelston Mill**. Go to the left of the cottages and through a gate to reach the river. Follow the river bank to reach a girder bridge that once carried a railway line, but now carries the Bitton to Bath Cycle Way. Go up to the cycle way and follow it leftwards to the next bridge, or go under the bridge, staying with the river to reach the next bridge. Now go under the bridge, or down off it, to follow a path that leads away from the river towards Kelston village. When a stream is reached bear half-right on a path that heads towards a farm. Go through a gate next to a thatched cottage to reach a lane that leads back to the church.

POINTS OF INTEREST:
Little Down Hillfort – The hillfort dates from the Iron Age when local tribes needed places to live or go if danger threatened. The forts were placed on hill tops or cliff edges so that these natural defences could be added to the man-made ditches and ramparts. Here the Cotswold edge defends the fort on two of its three sides. Little Down is an early hillfort, with just a single line of defences. Later, after the sling shot had been invented, multiple ditches were needed.

North Stoke – St Martin's Church is part Norman and part 19th century, extensive restoration work having been required to counter the ravages of time. The church houses an early Norman font.

Kelston Mill – During the 18th century this area of the Avon Valley was famous for its foundries. Kelston Mill was constructed as a brass foundry, the owner anticipating using an Avon driven waterwheel to operate his forge hammers. Sadly he went bankrupt before the Mill was fully operational.

REFRESHMENTS:
The Old Crown Inn, Kelston.

Walk 90   **RALEGH'S CROSS**   7m (11km)

Maps: OS Sheets Landranger 181; Pathfinder SS 03/13.

A walk along the high Brendon Hill ridge.

Start: At 039344, the Ralegh's Cross Inn.

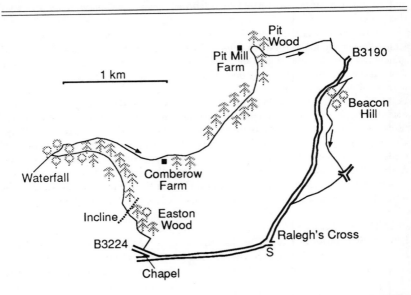

Walk west along the verge beside the B3190 to reach a **chapel** at a Y-junction. Here go right on the B3224 towards Wheddon Cross for 150 yards to reach a gate on the right. Go through and take the signed bridlepath beyond towards Eastern Wood. The bridlepath runs along a hedge: follow it, bearing left to reach a gate at the forest edge. Go through and follow a track beside the forest to reach a gate by an old shed. Go through to reach a path that goes steeply down to reach a red waymarked track near an **incline**. Go over the incline and follow the path across steep wooded slopes. Go through a gate and downhill to reach a signpost. Turn left here and follow the path to a 50 foot (16 metre) waterfall which hurls itself over a rocky outcrop.

    Beyond the waterfall the path contours around two combes to reach a fork. Go right on the path for Camberow Farm which is passed to its left. Go over a stream and turn left along an old railway track signed for Roadwater, following it towards Pitt

Mill Farm. Just before the farm go right, off the railway track and follow a path up through woods to reach a yellow waymarked path. Turn right along this, following it to a lane. Go right along the lane to reach the B3190.

Turn right along the road for 250 yards to reach, to the left, a path signed for Monksilver and Ralegh's Cross. Take this path and after 100 yards, at a path junction, go sharp right on a red waymarked path that rises across the wooded flank of Brecon Hill. The path bears left and climbs over a ridge then descends to reach a road, Colton Lane, at a point where the lane turns left. Here turn right on to a path signed for Ralegh's Cross. Follow this across several fields to reach the B3190 again. Turn left and walk down to **Ralegh's Cross** and the start of the walk.

POINTS OF INTEREST:

Chapel – The building at the road fork is a Methodist Beulah Chapel, built in 1861 for the Welsh and Cornish miners who had been brought to the Brendon Hills to work the iron ore mines.

Incline – The Brendon Hills Iron Ore Company was a rich one, having 31 shafts on the hills and, at its peak, around 1877, producing almost 50,000 tons of ore annually. But there was a real problem when it came to exporting the ore. To solve the problem a gravity railway was built down the hillside, linking with a railway to the port at Watchet. The incline dropped over $1/_2$ mile at a gradient of 1 in 4 and was powered by gravity, the full, descending, ore truck pulling up an empty truck, the whole being controlled by an 18 foot diameter cable drum that also acted as a brake. Some idea of the engineering required to produce the incline can be gauged by following it for a while. It is quite remarkably steep. It is planned to restore some of the mining equipment soon.

Ralegh's Cross – The plinth of the old stone cross that marked this ridge top junction can still be seen. It is not clear why the cross was so-called, but legend has it that the body of Simon de Ralegh, who had been killed in France in 1377, was rested here as it was being returned to his estate at Nettlecombe.

REFRESHMENTS:
The Ralegh's Cross Inn.

Walk 91   **BRIDGWATER BAY**   7m (11km)

Maps: OS Sheets Landranger 181; Pathfinder ST 04/14.

A walk where the Quantocks meet the sea.

Start: At 147439, Kilve church.

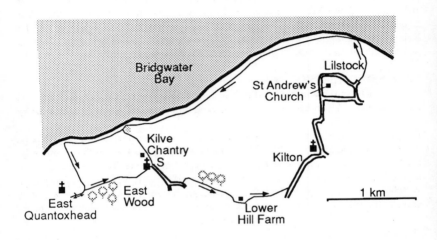

Go south along Sea Lane to reach Meadow House, to the right. Opposite the house go left up Hilltop Lane. Where the lane bears right go ahead on to an enclosed path and follow it to a gate. Go through, and follow the signed footpath which goes right to reach a footbridge over a stream. Go over a stile and cross a field with a copse of oak trees and the stream to the left. Go over two more stiles, staying with the copse. At its end go over the stile to the right and head for the old and new buildings of Lower Hill farm. Go left at the farm to reach a gate. Cross two large fields, then a smaller one to reach a road. Go left along it into Kilton.

At the next road junction go left, passing Kilton church to the left. Go around a prominent Z-bend, then go uphill slightly, ignoring a turn to the right, to reach St Andrew's church – also to the right, up a short green lane. Stay with the road as it bears right, then right again to the hamlet of Lilstock. Go past Lilstock farm to reach a T-junction. Go left here and walk past the road end car park to reach the sea.

Follow the cliff top path, dropping down to search for **fossils** on the beach if you wish, all the way to **Kilve Pill** where there is a permanent pond. The path inland from here offers a quick return to the start, but the better return is to continue for another 750 yards to where the path turns inland. Stay with it to reach, about 600 yards from the sea, a T-junction of paths. Go right into **East Quantoxhead**. After a look around the village return to the T-junction, but now head away from the village on a path that crosses fields at the edge of **East Wood**. At the wood end bear half-right to reach a gate in the middle of the opposite hedge. Go through and cross the field ahead to reach a gate into **Kilve** churchyard, and the start of the walk.

POINTS OF INTEREST:

Fossils – The Liassic limestone of the beach here is a recurrence of the Lyme Regis strata and is excellent for fossils, particularly ammonites. But please be careful if you are tempted to go near the cliffs – they are very unstable.

Kilve Pill – In earlier years this was a favourite spot for 'glatting' the searching for conger eels with dogs at very low tides. As the eels could be 10 feet long, with teeth and tempers to match, it was not for the faint-hearted.

East Quantoxhead – St Mary's Church is 15th century and has a stained glass window to the memory of Alexander Luttrell, rector for over 70 years.

East Wood – The wood was one of William Wordsworth's favourite spots when he lived locally, and is featured in several of his poems.

Kilve – The most interesting building in the village is not the church – though that is a fine place – but the ivy-clad ruin of Kilve Chantry to the north. It was founded by Simon de Furneaux in 1329, one of the duties of the five monks being to say verses for the souls of Simon, his wife and their heirs. When the property passed to Sir Richard Stury – who married a Furneaux heiress – he had it closed, thus cheating Henry VIII of the privilege. Some say Stury was opposed to the idea of the masses, being a follower of John Wycliff, the Lollard. Others say that Stury preferred to spend his wife's money on himself. The chantry was then used as a hay store, but caught fire when it was being used by smugglers as a brandy store. Not surprisingly it burned well.

Kilve church has stained glass windows which depict Joseph of Aramathea's trip to Glastonbury, and the sprouting of the Holy Thorn.

REFRESHMENTS:

None on route, but the Hood Arms in the main village of Kilve, a mile or so south of the church, can be used.

Walk 92   **TORMARTON AND DYRHAM**   7¹/₂m (12km)
Maps: OS Sheets Landranger 172; Pathfinder ST 67/77.
A section of the Cotswold Way, with a return over the South Wolds.
Start: At 769789, the Church in Tormarton.

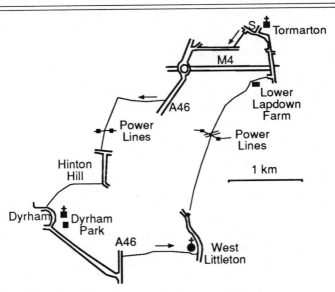

Tormarton Church is on the Cotswold Way, the Way continuing down to the village Post Office. Turn right to reach the Portcullis Inn, going left just beyond it on to a drive which soon reaches a stile. Go over and cross the field ahead to another stile. Go over and turn left to reach a third. Do not cross this: instead, turn right and follow the wall on the left to reach a road. Turn right and follow the road to another. Turn left on to this road to reach the main A46. Turn left and follow the main road's verge to reach the roundabout above the M4. You must now get to the far side of the roundabout, taking the verge of the A46 to Bath. At a lay-by follow the Cotswold Way marker which urges you to cross the road to another lay-by. Continue along the verge, then go right to a picnic area.

Follow the Cotswold Way markers from the picnic area to reach a narrow section

174

of woodland. Follow a field edge beyond the wood to reach a gate in a corner. Do not go through: instead, turn left and follow the hedge on the right to reach a lane at a T-junction. Cross to reach Field Lane and follow this to where it bends sharply left. Here go right and follow the Way along a bridleway, going through four gates, with **Hinton Hill** beyond the wall to your right. A short lane leads to the road in Dyrham village. Turn left to reach the church and an entrance to **Dyrham Park**.

Our walk leaves the Cotswold Way here, following a lane sharply uphill to reach the A46. Turn left along the road verge to reach the wall of Dyrham Park. Opposite, a signed path leads through a gate. Go across two fields, then cross a stream by way of a stone footbridge. Cross another field to reach the obvious landmark of West Littleton church. At the village road beyond the church, turn left. Follow the road for about 500 yards to reach a signed lane for Tormarton, to the right. Follow this and the path beyond, going under power lines to reach a road. Cross to reach a signed path opposite, heading for the right-hand corner of a field. Go half-right and follow the field edge to Lower Lapdown Farm. Take the farm lane to a road and turn left. This road crosses the M4 motorway to reach the village of Tormarton. Take the main road through the village as it bends left to reach the Post Office. Now go right to regain the church.

POINTS OF INTEREST:

Tormarton Church – There are Saxon stones in the tower of this late Norman church. Externally the most unusual feature is a pair of string courses on the east chancel wall. The lower of the two is of a type which is often seen. The upper one is of a form known as 'wheat-ear' and the only other known example in England is on Norwich Cathedral. Inside there is a superb brass to John Ceysill who died in 1493 and an extraordinary memorial to Edward Tapp, a lord of the manor, who died in 1699. Topp's coat-of-arms consisted of a nailed fist clutching a severed arm.

Hinton Hill – In 577 the Saxons defeated the Celts on the flank of this hill thus cutting off the Celts of the south-west from those of Wales. This was one of the most significant battles in English history, laying the foundation for the creation of Celtic Wales and the Celtic enclave of Cornwall.

Dyrham Park – The fine house was built by William Blathwayt, Secretary of War under William III, in the late 17th century. Blathwayt also had the Park laid out, the landscaping including a remarkable water garden with a 20-foot water jet fed by a lake. The house and park are a National Trust property.

REFRESHMENTS:
The Portcullis Inn, Tormarton.
The Crown Inn, Dyrham.

Walk 93   **THE GORDANO VALLEY**   8m (13km)

Maps: OS Sheets Landranger 172; Pathfinder ST 47/57.

Out along a wide valley, then back along the coast.

Start: At 4091727, St Mary's Church, Clevedon.

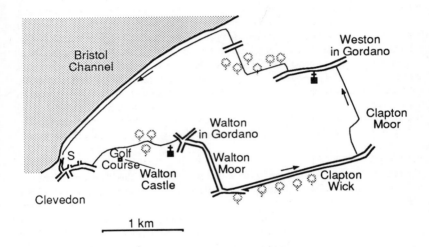

To reach the start point follow the sea front road northward from the remains of Clevedon's pier to reach the Church.

Take Castle Road from the church, following it for about 400 yards to reach, on the left, a turning for Clevedon Golf Course. Walk up the road, but leave it when it bears left to reach the club house, going straight ahead on a path signed for Walton-in-Gordano which heads off across the course. On this stretch you will need to keep a sharp lookout for the odd golf ball whizzing in your general direction.

Soon the artillery barrage is over, the path edging wooded Castle Hill – **Walton Castle** itself stands to the right – then dropping down to reach Walton-in-Gordano where the village church acts as a landmark. After passing through a small wooded area the path crosses open land to reach the churchyard. Take the lane beside the church to reach the main village street. Turn right to reach the B3124, the main

Gordano Valley road. Cross and take Moor Lane across Walton Moor. At the T-junction turn left and follow another lane to Clapton Wick. The lane through the strung out village moves in close under the M5 motorway. At the closest approach look for a signed path on the left. If you reach Wynhol Farm you have gone a few yards too far! The path goes through gates and also crosses several drainage ditches (or rhines, pronounced *reen*, as they are called locally). As it crosses Clapton Moor, the path bears right, then back left to cross a substantial rhine, then heads for a more defined track which is followed to the B3124 valley road in Weston-in-Gordano. Turn left and follow the main road out of the village. About 300 yards beyond the church go right on a signed path towards the hillside woods. Go left along the wood edge to reach a junction of paths. Now turn right through the wood, frightening a few cackling pheasants skyward at the right time of year.

The woodland path reaches a lane: follow this to a road. Cross the road on to a signed path that goes downhill to reach the cliff edge. Turn left along the coastal path at the cliff edge, admiring the view of the Bristol Channel and the Welsh Coast on your walk to **Clevedon**. This coastal section of the path is very clear and leads around Lodge Point to Lodge Bay. Here take the steps to the left to reach Bay Road, which leads back to the start point.

POINTS OF INTEREST:

Walton Castle – Despite the name the Castle was never a fortress. In fact it is a 17th century hunting lodge. In form it is octagonal, in style Gothic. Today it is a private house and is **not** on a right of way.

Gordano Valley – The name Gordano defies expert interpretation, though most likely it is from '*gore*', a wedge-shaped valley and *dene*, a small valley. That seems to have too many valley references, but there is no better explanation. Walton church is not particularly attractive, but Weston Church has an interesting bust of Spencer Percival, the only Prime Minister to have been assassinated, who came from a local family.

Clevedon – Clevedon is an elegant little town with a part restored pier which collapsed, in 1970, during the performance of a safety test! It stood, somewhat forlornly, in two pieces for several years until a restoration fund was set up. Sir John Betjeman even included a plea for it in one of his poems.

REFRESHMENTS:

The White Hart, Weston-in Gordano.

The Post Office in Walton-in-Gordano sells drinks and snacks, and there are numerous possibilities in Clevedon.

Walk 94   **SIMONSBATH**   8m (13km)

Maps: OS Sheets Landranger 180 and 181; Pathfinder SS 63/73 and SS 83/93.

A beautiful walk along the River Barle.

Start: At 774395, the Ashcombe car park/picnic site, Simonsbath.

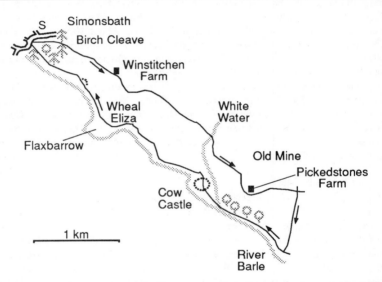

The car park is signed down a lane beside the church. Return to the main road (the B3358) and turn right. Pass the Exmoor Forest Hotel and cross to Pound Cottage. Beyond is a gate. Go through to reach a path that is waymarked in red, and signed for Landacre via Picked Stones. Follow the path through Birch Cleave, turning left close to its end to reach a gate (on the right). Go through the gate to open country and follow the fence to the left. Go across three further fields, the route waymarked in red at each boundary, to reach Winstitchen Farm. At a walled bank near the farm bear right and walk along it to reach a gate. Bear left through the gate and follow the left fence through two fields going along the line of the old **herepath**. In the third field the path goes to the right of a small conifer plantation to reach a gate. Go through and turn right downhill to reach White Water, a large tributary of the River Barle. To the right here, beside the small quarry, is the ruin of William Burgess' cottage (*see* Note on Wheal Eliza).

Cross the footbridge over White Water and go right along the path. The gruffy ground to the left is all that remains of the **Pickedstones Iron Mine**. The path goes through the yard of Pickedstones Farm to reach the farm road. Go along this away from the farm to reach a red marked gate on the right. Go through on to open moor and follow the path for 300 yards to reach a junction of paths at a red post. Here the main path continues ahead, but we turn right, downhill towards the River Barle. After 800 yards another path junction is reached, the Two Moors Way (*see* Note to Walk 98) crossing from left to right. Go right, along the Way, following the bank of the River Barle. A large conifer plantation is entered through a gate, and left through another, to reach a ford across the Barle. Do not cross: instead bear right to reach a footbridge over White Water and climb steeply up to **Cow Castle**. Cross the hillfort and go down the far side to a stile. Go over and follow the Barle's bank all the way to the remains of **Wheal Eliza** mine where the Barle is bridged. Here the path bears right, away from the river to round Flexbarrow, a natural mound. Beyond the mound the path returns to the river bank to reach a rocky outcrop. Beyond this the path bears away from the river to reach a gate into Birch Cleave. Go through and walk through the wood to reach the outward route at the road in Simonsbath. Go right to return to the start.

POINTS OF INTEREST:

Herepath – This ancient track linked Cornwall with the Midlands. The name is Saxon and means 'army road', though it is likely that the track pre-dated the Saxon conquest.
Pickedstones Iron Mine – The mine was worked from 1910 until 1914, but was never prosperous, the poor quality of the ore and the difficulties of transporting it causing its early shutdown.
Cow Castle – This natural mound is topped by an Iron Age hillfort.
Wheal Eliza – Both iron and copper were mined at the mine, though it is more famous for its part in one of Exmoor's most notorious crimes. William Burgess, a widower living near White Water, killed his daughter because she objected to his proposed remarriage and buried her on the moor. When searching parties looked as though they might find the body Burgess dug it up and threw it down a mineshaft, fleeing to Wales. The body was discovered, Burgess was arrested and hanged in Taunton jail in 1858.

REFRESHMENTS:
Simonsbath House Hotel, Simonsbath.
Exmoor House Hotel, Simonsbath.

Walk 95   **MELLS**   8m (13km)

Maps: OS Sheets Landranger 183; Pathfinder ST 64/74 and ST 65/75.

A fine walk on the eastern Mendips.

Start: At 728492, the church in Mells.

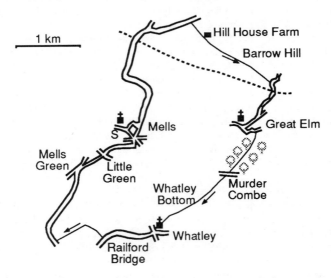

Go north from **Mells Church,** going along an avenue of the yews to reach a stile out of the churchyard. Cross a field to a gate, go through and cross another field to a gate on to a road. Bear left, quickly rounding a sharp right corner and staying on the road as it crosses a railway line. At a road junction go right, along Collier's Lane, following it to reach the lane, to the right, to Hill House Farm. Go down the lane and pass to the right of the buildings to reach an enclosed path on to Barrow Hill. To the left is an old colliery chimney. Where the enclosed path ends continue over the hill to reach a stile. Go over and head for the right side of the wood ahead. Go along the wood edge and cross a stile. Now follow the hedge to reach another enclosed path and follow this to a road. Go right, walking under the railway again. At a T-junction turn right into the village of Great Elm.

In Great Elm take the first turn left opposite the church and go downhill to the Mells Stream. Go sharp left at the bottom of the road, bearing right to cross a bridge over the stream. Now go right on to a path that follows the wooded stream valley. The path stays close to the stream all the way to the road in Murder Combe. Go left for a few yards, then cross to reach a path that runs along the left edge of a field above Whatley Bottom. Go through a gate and cross another field, heading towards the church and rectory of the hamlet of Whatley. Go over a stile into the churchyard.

Go through the churchyard and on to the road near a cross-roads. Our route heads west, towards Chantry, crossing Railford Bridge over the stream followed above Whatley Bottom. Beyond the bridge go over a stile on the right and follow the stream for a short while until a smaller bridge is reached. Bear left along this small stream to reach a stile. Go over and follow the stream and hedge to reach a gate on to a road. Go right and follow the road to Mells Green where there is a cross-roads. Bear right here, through Little Green, towards **Mells**. Go over at the next cross-roads following a road that bends sharply left to cross the **Mells Stream**. Beyond is the junction of five roads. Take the second left to return to the start of the walk.

POINTS OF INTEREST:

Mells Church – The 15th century church of St Andrew is a beautiful example of Somerset Perpendicular architecture. Inside, the Horner Chapel houses memorials to the famous Horner family (see below). In the churchyard are the graves of Siegfried Sassoon and Lady Violet Bonham-Carter, and two gravestones – of Sir John Horner and his wife – which were designed by Sir Edward Lutyens.

Mells – This is one of Somerset's prettiest villages and probably the basis for one of Britain's most endearing nursery rhymes. The village was held by Glastonbury Abbey, but at the Dissolution passed to the Horner family when Jack Horner, a steward to the Abbot, stole the deeds to the manor from a bundle of deeds he was carrying to London. The 'plum' of Mells therefore became Little Jack Horner's, and the nursery rhyme was born. Of course there are those who say that this is nonsense ...

Mells Stream – The stream was once the power source for Fussell's Ironworks, the greatest of Somerset's industrial complexes.

REFRESHMENTS:
The Talbot Inn, Mells.

Walk 96   DUNKERTON AND ENGLISHCOMBE   8m (13km)

Maps: OS Sheets Landranger 172; Pathfinder ST 65/75 and ST 66/76.

A ramble through the unspoilt country of old Somerset.

Start: At 716628, the church in Englishcombe.

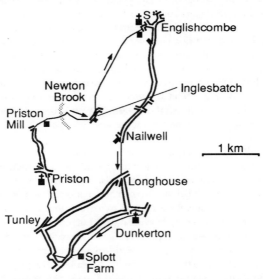

From **Englishcombe** church head south on the road for Priston, bearing right at a junction after 500 yards and following the road for a further 1¼ mile (2kms) to reach the hamlet of Nailwell. At the hamlet go left into a cul-de-sac near **Nailwell House**. When the road ends a footpath to the right continues southward, climbing across the flank of Duncorn Hill to reach a track on to a road, the B3115, at Longhouse. Cross the road, turn right, and then immediately left into a lane that goes steeply downhill towards Dunkerton, reaching the village after passing the remains of an old coal-carrying railway. At a T-junction go left, then right to reach **Dunkerton** church. Go to the left of the churchyard to reach a stile on the right. Go over and follow the path which runs close to the Cam Brook, on the right. The path crosses several fields, but is always obvious, and never very far away.

As the oddly-named Splott Farm is approached, do not cross a concrete bridge over the Brook. Instead, go over a stile and walk ahead to reach a road. Go left for 100 yards to reach a signed path on the left. This path also stays close to Cam Brook on the other side of which is a reclaimed slag heap from one of the area's old coal mines. Cross the Brook by a bridge and bear left to reach a road. Go right, uphill, to the hamlet of Tunley, through which runs the B3115. Cross and go left, then immediately right on a track which runs along the back of the hamlet's houses. Follow the track to where it ends at a gate. Go left on a path across open land to reach a stile. Go over and turn right, then immediately left on a downhill path to reach a stile to the right of a house. Go over on to a metalled lane and follow it to a road. Turn right to reach Priston. Go left at a T-junction, going through the village to reach a road junction. Go right on the road for **Priston Mill**. At a T-junction go right again to reach the Mill.

Go through the Mill's yard to reach a stile. Go over and follow the path towards Inglesbatch which can be seen up ahead. Go through the first field to reach a stream, following it until a footbridge gives access to a field. Follow the right boundary for 20 yards to reach a stile. Go over and walk uphill, following the line of the power cable to reach a rough track. Follow the track into Inglesbatch hamlet. Turn left at the telephone box and go through the hamlet to reach a junction of five lanes (including the one you are on). You want the second on the left, which heads due north. Take this and follow it downhill. When it ends take the path across delightful country, crossing a stream on a wooden bridge then climbing to reach a lane. Follow the lane back to Englishcombe church and the start of the walk.

POINTS OF INTEREST:

Englishcombe – The village is set on the Wansdyke, a little understood defensive earthwork probably built by the Celts against the Saxons, and probably extending from the Bristol Channel to Malrborough. Close by is Culverhay Castle, a massive earthwork probably associated with the dyke.

Dunkerton – Once a mining village, as were many of the local villages. The Somerset coal field was difficult to work, and the last mine closed about 25 years ago.

Priston Mill – A mill on this site was mentioned in the Domesday Book, though the present building is 18th century. The mill is powered by a 19th century waterwheel 28 foot in diameter. Unusually, the waterwheel is inside the mill. The mill is open to visitors on weekday afternoons, Sundays and Bank Holidays.

REFRESHMENTS:
The Ring o' Bells, Priston.
The Miller's Kitchen, Priston Mill.

Walk 97   THE WEST MENDIP WAY   8½m (13½km)

Maps: OS Sheets Landranger 182, Pathfinder ST 44/54 and ST 45/55.

The final section of this interesting trip.

Start: At 478509, the Card Memorial in Draycott.

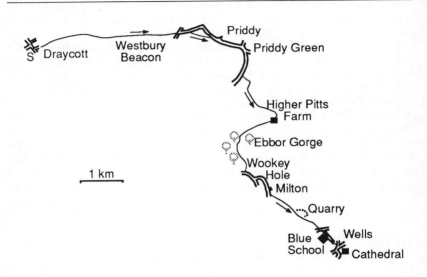

This straight line walk follows the final section of the 30 mile West Mendip Way, which runs the length of the Mendips, from Uphill to Wells. There is ample parking in Wells from where buses run along the main A371 to Cheddar and Axbridge. Take the bus and get off at Draycott.

From the **Card Memorial**, Draycott go uphill along The Batch, bearing right towards Swan Lane, then left up Sun Batch. The lane soon becomes a track. Go over a stile and walk along the wall to the right. At the end of the field go east over the hill, going over two stiles to meet a wall. Walk with this on your right hand to reach a stile. Continue across several fields, passing to the right of a tumulus and a pond, then crossing a field to reach a wall. Follow the wall to reach a gate on to a road. Cross the road to reach another, Caxton End Lane, for Priddy. Go along the road for 400 yards, then go right into a field. Turn left immediately into another field. Go across this and the one beyond to reach a road. Turn right into Priddy.

Go past Priddy Green, to the left, and the New Inn, to the right, following the road for Wookey Hole around to the right. Pass the Queen Victoria Inn and continue along the road to reach a signed path over a stile on the left. Go over the stile and walk along the wall on the left, following it when it turns to the right. Cross a stile, and stay with the wall until a stile in it allows you to change sides. Continue, with the wall now on your right. At a stile go over into Dursdon Drove, and turn left along it. Turn right into Higher Pitts Farm, going to the right of the buildings.

Bear left beyond the farm, then follow the fence on the right, staying with it when it bears right. Go across fields to reach the Ebbor Gorge Nature Reserve and follow a stepped path steeply down. Ignore a path off right, signed for Ebbor Gorge and its car park, and follow the path to a road. Go left and pass the Wookey Hole complex. Continue along the road, passing School Lane and Milton Lane, both to the left. Beyond Milton Lane a Waymarker points the way, to the left, along a field edge. Cross two fields, then go left and climb steeply to reach a stile into woods. The Way now visits Arthur's Point – a legendary look-out of King Arthur – before turning down through the wood again. Cross a stile and go left by the quarry to reach a metalled lane. Go over a stile to reach a path and follow it down to a road. Cross Ash Lane and continue through the Blue School. Go left along Lower's Walk, then right to reach the centre of **Wells**.

POINTS OF INTEREST:

Card Memorial – The memorial commemorates John Card, a Draycott resident who died in 1729 and left land and money to the village.

Wells – England's smallest city is dominated by its cathedral, one of the most beautiful in the country. The earliest church on the site was founded by St Aldhelm in 707, the present cathedral dating from the late 12th century. The west front is particularly magnificent, with over 300 statues in its niched walls. Close to the cathedral is the 13th century Bishop's Palace, the finest in Britain. The Palace is moated and has a drawbridge and, famously, swans on the moat ring a bell to be fed.

REFRESHMENTS:

The Red Lion, Wells Road, Draycott.
The Strawberry Special, Station Road, Draycott.
The New Inn, Priddy.
The Queen Victoria, Priddy.
There are also numerous possibilities in Wells.

Walk 98   **TARR STEPS**   9m (14^1/$_2$km)

Maps: OS Sheets Landranger 181; Pathfinder SS 83/93.

A walk past an enigmatic bridge.

Start: At 872324, the car park near Tarr Steps.

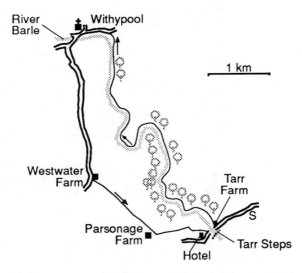

The bridge of Tarr Steps crosses the River Barle, but takes pedestrians only. It is approached by roads from both sides of the river, but the road from the west (from Hawkridge) does not allow the car park to be reached. To reach the start the road from the east (from Winsford or Dulverton via Liscombe) must be used.

From the car park go down the road towards **Tarr Steps**, but a few yards before the bridge go right at Tarr Farm taking either the bridleway just before it, or the footpath just after. Each of these routes is waymarked for the **Two Moors Way**, and they join beyond the farm. The route now is straightforward, following the River Barle's eastern bank – and only rarely moving more than a few yards away from it – and being well waymarked. Because the route is so close to the river the scenery is exquisite, but after heavy rain can be difficult.

As the route nears the village of Withypool it goes over four stiles in quick succession, the last one on to a road. Go left, into **Withypool**. Go through the village on the road for Hawkridge, and follow it for $1^1/_2$ miles ($2^1/_2$km) to reach Westwater Farm, on the left. Go past the farm and over a stream, then turn left on the waymarked path (this is an alternative section of the Two Moors Way). The path heads south-east, crossing several fields to reach Parsonage Farm. There the path bears left along the field edge going through two gates. In the third field a gap on the right leads to a track that is followed to a road. Go left to reach Tarr Steps and cross them to reach the outward route which is followed back to the start.

POINTS OF INTEREST:

Tarr Steps – The Steps are one of Exmoor's great mysteries, because no one knows how old they are. In 1968 the Post Office used them on a stamp, boldly labelling it 'prehistoric', since when most local guides have given the same information. It is likely, though, that they are contemporary with other clapper bridges – of which there are many, mostly on Dartmoor – which would make them medieval, probably 13th or 14th century. Clapper bridges were made by placing flat slabs of stone on rough pillars, and that is how Tarr Steps were made. But they are very big for a clapper – the largest slab is 7 x 4 ft (2m x $1^1/_4$m) and weighs several tons, and the whole bridge comprises 17 slabs and is 120 ft (36m) long – and the River Barle can be successfully forded beside the Steps for most of the year. Even when it cannot be forded there is another bridge only a mile or so to the south. Hence the mystery.

To add to the confusion the name could be from *tor* – as in Dartmoor tor – or *tochor*, a causeway, and which again adds a clue to the age. The only certain thing is that the clapper has been rebuilt several times after floods wrecked it, most recently in 1952.

Two Moors Way – The Way is a fine route, though not an official National Trail, which crosses Exmoor and Dartmoor's eastern flank in linking Lynmouth to Ivybridge.
Withypool – Under the Normans this village was the capital of Exmoor. The Royal Oak has had some famous visitors. Blackmoor wrote part of *Lorna Doone* here and General Eisenhower drank there, having arrived on horseback, after watching US troops training locally for D-Day.

REFRESHMENTS:
The Royal Oak, Withypool.
Tarr Farm offers teas and snacks during the summer months.

Walk 99   **MUCHELNEY ABBEY**   10m (16km)

Maps: OS Sheets Landranger 193; Pathfinder ST 42/52.
A long walk across the Somerset Levels.
Start: The Cocklemoor car park, Langport.

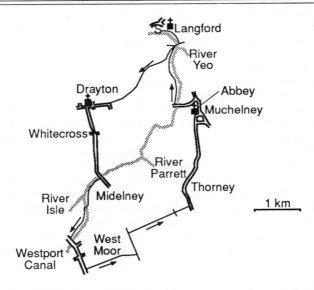

The car park lies behind Langport's main shopping centre, close to the northern bank
of the River Parrett.

Go out of the car park, cross the footbridge and go left along the River Parrett's
northern bank to reach Huish Bridge. Go over the bridge and walk forward to reach,
shortly, a gate on the left, signed for Muchelney and Drayton. Go through and turn
half-right across a field to reach a gate on to a lane. Go left to reach a gate. Go through
and immediately turn right through a gate. Follow the right-hand hedge across a field
and cross a rhine by the double gates. Go through a gate to cross an old railway track.
Go through the gate on the opposite side and cross the field to a gate in the far hedge.
Go through and turn half-left to cross a field into its far corner. Go over some rails and
turn half-right to a gate. Go through and cross the field beyond to a stile. Go over and
diagonally across a field to a gate beside trees. Go through to an enclosed path to

reach a road at a sharp bend. Go along the road into Drayton.

Walk past the church and turn left. At a road junction go ahead on the No Through Road to **Midelney**. Before the village is reached the road crosses the River Isle. Go over the bridge and turn right on to the path along the river bank. After 400 yards the **Westport Canal** is reached, the path following its bank. At a bridge the path changes banks, but continues to follow the canal. Ignore the next footbridge, continuing to reach a road bridge. Turn left along the road for 100 yards to reach an old drove road on the left. Follow the drove for $^1/_2$ mile (800 metres) across **West Moor** to a path junction. Go leftt for 400 yards, then right at another path junction. Follow the new path, going straight ahead at another junction, to a road.

Turn left through Thorney and continue along the road, ignoring a right turn, and bearing left once, into **Muchelney**.

Turn left past the church, walking past the abbey and on along the road to reach Westover Bridge over the River Isle. Go over the bridge and turn right through a gate on a path signed for Huish Bridge. Follow the riverbank all the way to Huish Bridge and from there reverse the outward route back to the start.

POINTS OF INTEREST:

Midelney – A visit to Midelney Manor requires a 1 mile ($1^1/_2$km) detour, but is worthwhile as the Elizabethan manor is delightful. The site was originally owned by the Abbot of Muchelney, but after the Dissolution his country house was demolished and the present building erected.

Westover Canal – The canal was dug in the 1830s to link Westport with the River Parrett.

West Moor – This fine section of the Somerset Levels is popular with herons and plovers, and also has a good collection of marsh plants.

Muchelney – The abbey here was an 8th century foundation and was occupied by Benedictine monks. After its dissolution it became, as did so many others, a handy quarry for the locals, so that today little remains other than the foundation plan.

The village church is worth visiting to see the ceiling which was painted in the early 17th century with a curious scene of well-rounded cherubs and clouds. Opposite the church is the Priest's House, a National Trust property. This beautiful building is late medieval, with large Gothic windows and is delightfully furnished. The House is open by appointment.

REFRESHMENTS:

The Drayton Arms, Drayton.
There are also several possibilities in Langport.

Walk 100   **THE COTSWOLD WAY**   12m (19km)

Maps: OS Sheets Landranger 172; Pathfinder ST 66/76 and ST 67/77.

A fine walk following the last miles of the Cotswold Way.
Start: At 751728, Cold Ashton Church.

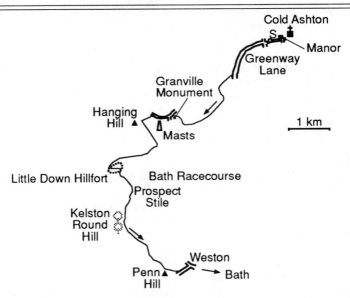

A bus service links Bath to Cold Ashton allowing day walkers to enjoy the final stage of the Cotswold Way, one of the most interesting of Britain's long-distance footpaths.

Go south through the churchyard to the village road. Turn right, passing Cold Ashton Manor (*see* Note to Walk 84). Where the village road bears right go straight on to reach the main A46. Cross to reach Greenway Lane. Follow the lane as it descends. About 100 yards beyond Hill Farm, the Cotswold Way goes right. Follow a path across three fields to reach a lane close to a cottage. Go left, crossing several cattle grids before a Cotswold Waymarker is found on the right. Leave the lane, fording a small stream and heading uphill. Cross a stile and continue uphill until a green lane is reached. Turn right and continue to climb. When the lane ends in a field, bear right and go uphill to reach a wall stile. Go over and follow the wall to the right.

Beyond the wall the Cotswold Way descends into a pleasant section of wood, going left when a wall is reached. Go over a stile and bear left to reach the **Granville Monument**. Walk on to the road. Cross it and follow the access road to the Monitoring Station whose masts can be seen ahead. Go to the right of the station, then turn left and follow the signed path. The path leads to the trig point on Hanging Hill, but the Cotswold Way goes sharp left over a stile before it is reached. Walk on to the golf course, taking a path through a clump of pine trees. Go left along a wood edge, then cross a drive to reach a path junction. Turn right and follow a bridleway going left, as directed by the waymark post. The Way now follows the edge of the Little Down hillfort to reach a stile on the left. Go over and cross the hillfort. At its far edge go right to reach a field corner. Turn left and walk past Bath racecourse to reach Prospect Stile where a panorama dial helps the walker identify the impressive view.

Cross the stile and go left. At a junction turn right, then go left, and finally right into a field. The Way is now obvious: there is even a section of boardwalk where it has become muddy. Soon Pendeen Farm is reached: go over a stile to the left of the house. Follow a wall to a stile, go over and follow a path to the trig point on Penn Hill. Cross two more stiles to reach a playing field and a road. Go left into the village of Weston. The old village church is reached by steps from High Street: from it go left, then right to reach Purlewent Drive. Go along it, then bear left into a cul-de-sac from where a footpath leads across Primrose Hill to reach a road. Cross and follow a path to Summerhill Road. Follow it, then go first right, into Sion Hill which soon goes round a 180° left hand bend. Complete most of this bend, then go right on a footpath over High Common. The path emerges on to Weston Road. Go left, then right at the cross-roads. After a few yards go left into Royal Crescent. Now follow Walk 4 to Bath Abbey.

POINTS OF INTEREST:

Granville Monument – On 5 July 1643 the Battle of Lansdown was fought between the Parliamentarian army of Sir William Waller and the Royalists under Sir Ralph Hopton and Prince Maurice. Waller took up a position at the northern end of the down, forcing the Royalists to charge uphill into the teeth of artillery fire. Just as it seemed the Royalists would be routed, Sir Bevil Granville led his Cornishmen up the hill. Inspired by Granville the Cornishmen forced Waller's men to retreat. But at the moment of victory Granville was wounded. He was taken to Cold Ashton Manor where he died. Waller and his army retreated to Bath, but two weeks later the city fell and it was the Cornishmen who lead the Royalist army into Bath.

REFRESHMENTS:
The White Hart, Cold Ashton.

Titles in the Series